Epicureanism

Ancient Philosophies

This series provides fresh and engaging new introductions to the major schools of philosophy of antiquity. Designed for students of philosophy and classics, the books offer clear and rigorous presentation of core ideas and lay the foundation for a thorough understanding of their subjects. Primary texts are handled in translation and the readers are provided with useful glossaries, chronologies and guides to the primary source material.

Published

The Ancient Commentators on Plato and Aristotle
Miira Tuominen

Ancient Scepticism
Harald Thorsrud

Cynics
William Desmond

Epicureanism
Tim O'Keefe

Neoplatonism
Pauliina Remes

Presocratics
James Warren

Stoicism
John Sellars

Forthcoming

Classical Islamic Philosophy
Deborah Black

Confucianism
Paul Goldin

Indian Buddhist Philosophy
Amber Carpenter

Plato
Andrew Mason

Socrates
Mark McPherran

Epicureanism

Tim O'Keefe

ACUMEN

For Mom and Dad

First published in 2010 by Acumen

Acumen Publishing Limited
4 Saddler Street
Durham
DH1 3NP
www.acumenpublishing.co.uk

ISBN: 978-1-84465-169-6 (hardcover)
ISBN: 978-1-84465-170-2 (paperback)

British Library Cataloguing-in-Publication Data
A catalogue record for this book is available
from the British Library.

Typeset in Minion.
Printed in the UK by the MPG Books Group.

Contents

Preface

Why to read this book

Epicurus' thought had a significant impact on the world: along with Stoicism and Academic Scepticism, Epicureanism was one of the major philosophical systems competing for the allegiance of thoughtful people in the Hellenistic world; Epicurean communities flourished for hundreds of years after Epicurus' death; and the rediscovery of Epicurus' philosophy helped shape the scientific revolution. Also, and in my view more importantly, Epicurus was a first-rate philosopher. He provides a systematic account of the nature of the world and our place in it, how we can come to know the world, and how we can attain happiness. Along the way he lays out arguments on a whole host of subsidiary topics, such as the nature of the mind and its relationship to the body, the untenability of scepticism, the development of society, the role friendship plays in attaining happiness, and the afterlife (or lack thereof). In my own experience, grappling with what Epicurus has to say about something has always helped sharpen and deepen my own thinking on that subject, even where I ended up concluding that he was deeply mistaken. Epicurus himself would claim that we should study him simply to attain happiness. According to Epicurus, a proper understanding of the workings of the world and the natural limits of our desire will free us from superstitious fears and allow us to attain an untroubled, blessed life.

But Epicurus' own writings are mostly lost to us, and what is left consists largely of summaries of his positions and short sayings, often written in a dense and jargon-laden style. The extended expositions of Epicurus' philosophy by Lucretius and Cicero are more informative and approachable, but even these can be deeply puzzling if used as starting-points for understanding Epicurus, since Lucretius and Cicero did not aim their writings at an audience of twenty-first-century English speakers. I hope that this book serves as a useful introduction to Epicurus' positions and the arguments he gives in favour of them.

How to use this book

This book is intended as a stand-alone introduction. I do not include extended quotations from ancient sources; instead, I usually summarize matters in my own words. However, I encourage interested readers to go back to the ancient texts themselves. I gather together a list of ancient readings on Epicureanism for each chapter at the end of the book. Some readers (or teachers) may wish to pair this book with a compendium of ancient texts. For these readers, I also include references to the two best compendia of texts on Epicureanism in English translation: the second edition of *Hellenistic Philosophy: Introductory Readings*, by Brad Inwood and Lloyd Gerson (1997) and *The Hellenistic Philosophers*, by A. A. Long and D. N. Sedley (1987). Many of the ancient texts I refer to are also in these compendia; where this is so, I indicate this using the following conventions: (IG <text number>) for Inwood and Gerson, (LS <text number>) for Long and Sedley.[1] In order to improve readability, in cases where I refer repeatedly in a chapter to passages from a single work – for instance, particular places within an extended stretch of Epicurus' *Letter to Herodotus* or Plutarch's *Against Colotes* – I have often omitted the IG and LS references in my parenthetical passage references within the chapter and included them only in the lists of ancient sources within the Further Reading. These lists of ancient sources include only those pertaining directly to Epicureanism; I have not collated the references to passages of, for example, Aristotle and Plato that I refer to along the way to help illuminate Epicureanism.

Lucretius is our best source for Epicurus' metaphysics and physics, as well as being a wonderful poet. Both LS and IG include some selections from Lucretius (LS much more extensively than IG). However, they (understandably) leave much out, given the length of Lucretius' poem, so some people may find it useful to read this book along with Lucretius too. Fortunately, a large number of good and reasonably priced translations of Lucretius are available. Three in particular I recommend: Martin Ferguson Smith's translation *On the Nature of Things* (2001) is accurate and readable, and includes useful notes. For those who want to read Lucretius' poetry as poetry, not prose, Rolfe Humphries' vigorous translation *The Way Things Are* (1968) is outstanding, albeit fairly free in its rendering of Lucretius, while A. E. Stallings's recent translation *The Nature of Things* (2007) is also quite good and closer to the text and tone of Lucretius. Many of Cicero's treatises are our best sources of information for key parts of Epicureanism. This is particularly true of his *De Finibus Bonorum et Malorum* (On ends), which reports Epicurus' ethics in book one and criticizes it in book two. Raphael Woolf gives a fine translation, accompanied by Julia Annas's (2001) extensive introduction.

I avoid extensive wrangling in scholarly controversy of the sort that is better done in journal articles, since doing so would quickly derail this book from its purpose. Instead, I just put forward what I myself take Epicurus' views to be, backed up by references to the texts, although I do sometimes indicate where what I say is controversial. Since my interpretations of Epicurus are not especially idiosyncratic, I do not think that the reader will be badly misled by this approach. However, the reader should be aware that many aspects of Epicurus' thought are controverted. I include Further Reading at the end of the book for readers who wish to explore scholarly issues further. Volume 2 of LS includes an excellent (if now dated) annotated bibliography, organized topically. And *The Cambridge Companion to Epicureanism* edited by James Warren (2009) aims to give insight into the current scholarship, and hence has an extensive bibliography.

Acknowledgements

I would like to thank the many students at the University of Minnesota, Morris, and at Georgia State University to whom I have taught bits and pieces of Epicureanism, particularly the students in my Epicurus class at Georgia State during autumn 2008. Interacting with all of you has helped immensely in writing this book.

I had the privilege of being on the committee for Kelly Arenson's dissertation on Epicurean pleasure, and of supervising Melissa Strahm's MA thesis on Epicurean friendship. Both of them improved my understanding and appreciation of Epicureanism.

Steven Gerrard has been an encouraging and patient editor, and the reviewers for Acumen gave detailed and useful feedback. Sylvia Berryman and Hal Thorsrud both looked over a draft of the complete manuscript and improved it in innumerable ways.

Anne Farrell has been a great sounding board and support throughout the writing process. Quinn, Brennan and Katie have shown me that the Epicureans might be right that children do not generally bring tranquillity, but they can give joy. I dedicate this book to my mom and dad. In their roles as Gammy and Pa, they stepped up and gave me the time I needed during a crucial stage of the composition of the book.

Tim O'Keefe
Decatur, Georgia

Sources and abbreviations

Athenaeus (Ath.)
Deipnosophists

Aristotle (Arist.)
Cael. = *De caelo*
Eth. Nic. = *Nicomachean Ethics*
Int. = *De interpretatione*
Metaph. = *Metaphysics*
Part. an. = *Parts of Animals*
Ph. = *Physics*

Cicero (Cic.)
Acad. = *Academica*
Fat. = *On Fate*
Fin. = *On Ends*
Nat. D. = *On the Nature of the Gods*

Diogenes Laertius
DL = *Lives of the Philosophers*

Epicurus
Ep. Hdt. = *Letter to Herodotus*
Ep. Men. = *Letter to Menoeceus*
Ep. Pyth. = *Letter to Pythocles*
KD = *Principal Doctrines*
VS = *Vatican Sayings*

Galen (Gal.)
On Medical Experience

Lactantius (Lactant.)
On the Anger of God

Lucretius
DRN = *On the Nature of Things (De rerum natura)*

Philodemus (Phld.)
Piet. = *On Piety*

Plato (Pl.)
Grg. = *Gorgias*
Hp. mai. = *Greater Hippias*
Men. = *Meno*
Phd. = *Phaedo*
Phlb. = *Philebus*
Rep. = *Republic*
Tht. = *Theatetus*
Ti. = *Timaeus*

Plutarch (Plut.)
Adv. Col. = *Against Colotes*
Non posse = *A Pleasant Life*
St. Rep. = *On Stoic Self-Contradictions*

Porphyry (Porph.)
Abst. = *On Abstinence*

Seneca (Sen.)
Ep. = *Letters*

Sextus Empiricus (Sext. Emp.)
Math. = *Against the Professors*
Pyr. = *Outlines of Pyrrhonism*

Simplicius (Simpl.)
in Phys. = *Commentary on Aristotle's Physics*

Stobaeus (Stob.)
Anthology

Theophrastus (Theophr.)
Sens. = *De sensibus*

Xenophon (Xen.)
Mem. = *Memorabilia*

Compendia

DK = *Die Fragmente der Vorsokratiker*, H. A. Diels & W. Kranz
IG = *Hellenistic Philosophy: Introductory Readings*, 2nd edn, Brad Inwood & Lloyd Gerson (1997)
LS = *The Hellenistic Philosophers*, A. A. Long & D. N. Sedley (1987)

Chronology

BCE	*c.*515–440	Parmenides
	*c.*460–370	Democritus
	*c.*429–347	Plato
	384–322	Aristotle
	*c.*365–270	Pyrrho
	341	Epicurus born in Samos
	334	Zeno of Citium born
	306	Epicurus founds the Garden in Athens
	*c.*301	Zeno of Citium founds the Stoic school in Athens
	271	Epicurus dies; Hermarchus assumes headship of the Garden
	*c.*268	Arcesilaus becomes head of the Academy and turns it in a sceptical direction
	262	Zeno of Citium dies
	214–129	Carneades
	*c.*110–40	Philodemus
	106–43	Cicero
	*c.*94–55	Lucretius
	early-mid 1st century	Aenesidemus founds Pyrrhonian scepticism
CE	*c.*50–120	Plutarch
	79	Mount Vesuvius erupts, burying Epicurean villa and library in Herculaneum
	2nd century	Sextus Empiricus
	late 2nd century	Diogenes of Oinoanda
	*c.*225	Diogenes Laertius composes *Lives and Opinions of the Philosophers*

ONE

Introduction: the life of Epicurus and the history of Epicureanism

Epicurus was born in 341 BCE in the Athenian colony of Samos, an island in the Mediterranean Sea near present-day Turkey. He began practising philosophy early, at the age of either twelve or fourteen, according to different reports. This interest was apparently spurred because of contempt for his schoolteachers. He wanted to understand what Hesiod meant when he claimed in the *Theogony* that first of all Chaos came into being, and from Chaos sprang Earth, Eros, Darkness and Night. When they were unable to interpret these lines for him, he turned to philosophy.

Epicurus said he was self-taught, but this claim is usually not taken seriously. The details of his early philosophical education are unclear, but he is said to have studied with Pamphilus, a follower of Plato (*c.*429–347 BCE), and (in a more reliable report) under Nausiphanes, a follower of Democritus (*c.*460–370 BCE), one of the inventors of atomism.

Even in the sketchy story above, we can discern many of the formative influences on Epicureanism. One of the main themes of Epicurus' philosophy is its resolute stand against the sort of destructive and retrograde superstition represented by Hesiod's theogony. Hesiod begins with a mythological account of the spawning of the universe from Chaos, and ends up with the triumph of the Olympian deities over their Titanic forebears. And with their triumph, these jealous beings, with superhuman powers and subhuman characters, are free to use us as pawns in their petty squabbles.

Epicurus lived in a time of great intellectual ferment, when the hold of traditional Greek religion, as promulgated in Hesiod and Homer, was weakened but not yet shattered. The first Greek philosophers (nowadays called the "Presocratics") proposed that phenomena such as earthquakes could be explained naturalistically, instead of being seen as the will of the gods. For instance, Anaximenes said that earthquakes were the result of the earth cracking as it dried out. This was rightfully seen as threatening by traditionalists. The philosopher Anaxagoras was reportedly banished from Athens for impiety because he said that the sun was a hot stone (instead of the chariot of Apollo), and Socrates was executed in 399 BCE in part because he denied the gods of the city. Plato's *Apology* and the unflattering portrayal of Socrates in Aristophanes' play *The Clouds* make it clear that one of the reasons people thought this of him is that he was (wrongly) viewed by some people as one of the "natural philosophers" who sought to replace the gods with elements such as air. And even in Epicurus' lifetime, Aristotle was indicted for impiety (although the charges were politically motivated) and fled Athens in 323 BCE (*DL* V 5–6).

One of the main sources of human unhappiness, according to Epicurus, is the fear fostered by such superstitious accounts of natural phenomena. In order to combat this fear, we must banish the meddling gods of popular religion by providing rational, naturalistic explanations in place of superstitious ones. This theme is given its strongest expression near the start of Lucretius' massive and magnificent poem *On the Nature of Things*, which sets forth Epicurean physics. Lucretius says that human beings were grovelling and crushed under the weight of superstition. But then Epicurus travelled through the measureless universe and discovered what could be and what could not, and with this knowledge trampled superstition underfoot and lifted us to the heavens (*DRN* I 62–79).

In order to combat these superstitions, Epicurus sought to revive the atomist philosophy of Democritus, according to which the basic constituents of the world are indivisible bits of matter (atoms) moving about in empty space (void), with all else being the result of the interactions of these atoms. But in order to do this, Epicurus needed to combat not only popular religion but also philosophical rivals of Democritus, chief among them Plato. Plato was no friend of popular Olympian religion either: dialogues such as the *Euthyphro* and the *Republic* make it clear that he regarded as sacrilegious its conception of flawed deities. But otherwise, Plato and Epicurus are opposed on almost every important matter; as a first approximation, one will not go far wrong in viewing Epicurus as the anti-Plato. Plato minimizes the role of the senses in gaining knowledge, whereas Epicurus holds that all knowledge is grounded in sense-experience. In his dialogue the *Timaeus*, Plato puts forward a picture of the world as the product of a beneficent deity, and says that the workings of the world must be explained in terms of how they are for the best, whereas Epicurus holds everything to be the fortuitous result of atoms blindly bumping and grinding in the void. Plato believes in an immaterial soul and an afterlife, in which the virtuous are rewarded and the vicious punished, whereas for Epicurus the soul is a conglomeration of atoms that ceases to exist on the death of the body, so that there is nothing for us to fear in death.

Epicurus regarded Democritus as a great philosopher, but he was no slavish adherent of Democritus. Instead, Democritean atomism had internal problems, which Epicurus sought to overcome. Chief among these are its latent scepticism and fatalism. Democritus regards sensible properties such as sweetness and redness as not really present in material objects at all, which seems to make the reports of the senses systematically misleading. Democritus himself seems dubious of whether we can gain knowledge of the world, and later followers of his declare flatly that we know nothing. Epicurus regarded such scepticism as untenable, and he wishes to show that atomism is consistent with the reality of sensible qualities and the reliability of the senses. And if what is going to happen in the future has been set from time immemorial by the past positions and motions of the atoms that make up the universe, this would seem to render what will happen necessary, and make our attempts to affect the future pointless. Epicurus wanted to demonstrate that atomism would not have such disastrous fatalistic consequences for our agency. Epicurus also needed to show that the atomist ambition of explaining everything from the "bottom up", in terms of the purposeless interactions of atoms in the void, was tenable. Plato's pupil Aristotle (384–322 BCE) had raised serious objections against Democritus on precisely this point, objections that Epicurus needed to overcome.

In one sense, Epicureanism is an intensely individualistic philosophy. Once we cast off the corrupting influences of superstition and society, we can recognize that the only thing that is valuable in itself is one's own pleasure. Anything else (including philosophy) is valuable only in so far as it helps one obtain pleasure for oneself. But at the same time, Epicureanism is a communal philosophy. Epicurus holds that the most pleasant life is a tranquil one, free of fear and need. We need the help of other people to attain this life. Wise individuals who recognize this can gather together and form communities in which they protect one another from the dangers of the outside world. Epicurus stresses the importance of friendship in attaining blessedness. Being part of a network of friends who can be trusted to help support one another in times of need is the greatest means for attaining tranquillity. Epicureanism is also an evangelical philosophy. Committed Epicureans thought that they had discovered a rational route to salvation, and they wished to spread the gospel of enlightened self-interest against the forces of superstition. Once again, Lucretius eloquently expresses this: the terrifying darkness that envelops our mind will be dispelled not by the rays of the sun, but only by a systematic account of the principles of nature (*DRN* I 146–8).

These aspects of Epicureanism are reflected in Epicurus' biography. After he had devised his philosophical system, he set up Epicurean communities in Mytilene and Lampsacus, before going to Athens around 306 BCE. At that time, Athens was the centre of the philosophical world, housing the schools founded by Plato and Aristotle, the Academy and the Lyceum, as well as other philosophical descendants of Socrates, such as the Cynics, Cyrenaics and Megarians. There, Epicurus established the Garden, which was a combination of philosophical school and community in which the members tried to put into practice the principles of Epicurean living. The Garden was surprisingly egalitarian, letting in women and people of all social classes.

Epicurus was renowned for his kindness to his many friends, a fact acknowledged even by his detractors, such as Cicero. Epicurus died in 271 BCE, after suffering from kidney stones for fourteen days. In a letter he wrote shortly before he died, he claimed that his joy at recollecting his discussions with his friends helped counterbalance his terrible physical suffering. He made careful provisions in his will for the continuation of the Epicurean communities, which included setting dates for celebrations commemorating his birthday and other important Epicureans.

Epicureanism proved highly influential, with Epicurean communities springing up throughout the Greek-speaking world. Despite its popularity, Epicureanism also sparked great enmity. Its denial of divine providence was deemed impious, and its advice that one should "live hidden" and avoid entanglement in politics was thought to undermine public order. And even though Epicurus said that limiting one's desires and living virtuously was the way to attain a pleasant life, Epicureanism was accused of undermining morality, and the Garden was allegedly the scene of debauched orgies.

With the rise of Christianity, Epicureanism went into decline. In the medieval period, the two primary sources of philosophical inspiration were Plato and Aristotle. The little attention that Epicurus received was usually in the service of criticizing atheistic materialism. However, Epicurean atomism was revived in the seventeenth century. The scientific revolution spurred a widespread reaction against the Aristotelian natural philosophy that had previously been dominant. Pierre Gassendi (1592–1655) and Robert Boyle (1627–91) both formulated versions of atomism explicitly based on Epicureanism, and they in turn had an influence on Isaac Newton (1643–1727). It is important to note that these thinkers tried to make their Epicurean atomism compatible with Christianity by restricting its application to the workings of the natural world, which does not include God, angels, the soul and the like.

Even many thinkers who were not atomists, such as René Descartes (1596–1650), had "mechanistic" natural philosophies that were, generally speaking, in sympathy with Epicureanism against Aristotelianism. Such thinkers rejected Epicurus' contentions that absolutely empty space is necessary for motion, and that there are smallest units of matter. Nonetheless, like Epicurus, they thought that natural processes could be explained simply in terms of the mechanical interactions of bits of extended stuff, with no recourse to purposes in nature or to irreducible powers.[1]

Most of the empirical claims Epicurus made about the world – some fundamental to his system, others peripheral – have since been falsified. Atoms are not indivisible and do not naturally fall straight downwards at uniform velocity, the mind is not located in the chest, and the bitter taste of some foods is not a result of rough and barbed particles tearing at the tongue. So it is not surprising that the philosophical system of Epicureanism has no adherents today. Nonetheless, many parts of the basic Epicurean worldview, broadly construed, are still very much live options. Epicurus holds that we can and must rely on the senses to gain knowledge of the universe and, when we do so, we discover a world without purpose or plan, indifferent to our concerns. We also discover that, like all other things, we are entirely material beings, and that death is annihilation. But this knowledge is not disheartening; instead, it liberates us from the superstitious fears of the gods and of death, and allows us to concentrate on attaining happiness here and now. And if we are wise, limiting our desires to what we really need and living in harmony with our friends, happiness is not difficult to attain. As the Epicurean Philodemus summarizes, in his "four-fold cure", "Nothing to fear from god, nothing to worry about in death. Good is easy to obtain, and evil easy to endure" (Phld. Herculaneum papyrus 1005, 4.9–14, LS 25J).

Sources on Epicureanism

Scholars studying Kant have to work hard to understand and interpret Kant's often difficult writing, but they have a complete corpus of

Kant's texts to work with. The project of trying to understand ancient philosophers is greatly complicated because we often have to work with sources that are not only obscure but fragmentary or unreliable. Among ancient philosophers, Epicurus occupies something of a middle ground when it comes to sources. Unlike Plato or Aristotle, we have fairly little of Epicurus' own writings, and some of the later sources (such as Cicero and Plutarch) have to be handled with care. But we do have a non-trivial amount of Epicurus' own writings, and the later sources (especially Lucretius and Cicero) often give quite extensive reports of the arguments in favour of Epicurean positions, which puts us in a better position to understand Epicurean philosophy than is the case for many ancient philosophers, such as the Cyrenaics and most of the Presocratics. Here are the major sources that will inform the subsequent account.

Epicurus himself

Unsurprisingly, Christians by and large were inimical to Epicurus, and even though he was a voluminous author (*DL* X 27–8), few of his writings survived the Middle Ages. Diogenes Laertius (fl. *c.* 3rd century CE) wrote a ten-book summary of the lives and doctrines of many Greek philosophers. This work has to be used cautiously, as Diogenes copies from various sources accounts of philosophers' doctrines and snippets of gossip about their lives with little regard for their accuracy. But Diogenes Laertius is nonetheless one of our best sources on Epicureanism, largely because the last book of his work, which deals with Epicurus, includes three letters Epicurus himself wrote: the *Letter to Herodotus*, which summarizes his metaphysics and physics; the *Letter to Pythocles*, which gives explanations of celestial and meteorological phenomena; and the *Letter to Menoeceus*, which summarizes his ethics. All three letters are valuable starting-points for understanding Epicurus, but all are only digests of major points, so many details and supporting argumentation are left out. Diogenes also preserves the *Principal Doctrines*: forty of Epicurus' sayings that deal mostly with ethical matters. The *Vatican Sayings* is a collection of quotations from Epicurus and his followers, some of which overlap the *Principal Doctrines*, preserved in a manuscript from the Vatican Library.

An Epicurean villa in the town of Herculaneum was buried by the eruption of Mount Vesuvius in 79 CE. The villa's library was unearthed in the eighteenth century, and work continues today in unrolling, deciphering, translating and interpreting the carbonized scrolls, which include portions of Epicurus' *magnum opus*, *On Nature*. Unfortunately, the texts are largely in terrible shape.

Later Epicureans

I have already mentioned the Roman poet Lucretius (*c.*94–55 BCE), whose six-book poem *De Rerum Natura* (On the nature of things) is our best source for Epicurus' metaphysics and physics: his arguments for the existence of atoms and void, and how to account for all other phenomena in atomistic terms. We know basically nothing about his life; a much later report that he was driven mad by a love potion and composed *On the Nature of Things* during lucid intervals is not credible. We also have considerable (although often fragmentary) remains of the work of Philodemus, an Epicurean philosopher of the first century BCE, which were uncovered in the Herculaneum villa. Near the end of his life, Diogenes of Oinoanda (second century CE) had extensive summaries of Epicurean teachings inscribed on portico walls in the city of Oinoanda (in modern-day central Turkey) in order to spread Epicurus' healing message to his fellow citizens, foreigners and future generations. The remains of this inscription were discovered in 1884.[2]

Other Epicureans are known to us only through the works of other, non-Epicurean philosophers. Colotes (fl *c.*310–260 BCE) was a younger compatriot of Epicurus who wrote the polemic *That it is Impossible Even to Live According to the Doctrines of the Other Philosophers*, spurring the spirited rejoinder *Against Colotes* by the Platonist philosopher and biographer Plutarch (*c.*50–120 CE). Hermarchus succeeded Epicurus as head of the Garden, and his account of the origin of justice and the reasons why we have no obligations of justice towards animals is quoted extensively by Porphyry (third-century CE Platonist and pupil of Plotinus) in *On Abstinence from Animal Food*, Porphyry's brief for vegetarianism.

The Epicureans had a reputation for doctrinal conservatism, inspired by their reverence for Epicurus, so these Epicureans probably did not depart far from Epicurus' thought. But they did not merely copy Epicurus. For one thing, they engaged in philosophical combat with new opponents that Epicurus did not target. Right around the time of Epicurus' death, Arcesilaus assumed the head of Plato's Academy and turned it in a sceptical direction, arguing that nothing can be known. Colotes makes the Academic Sceptics one of his primary foils when trying to show that anyone who casts doubt on the reliability of the senses thereby renders life impossible. Around 301 BCE, Zeno of Citium founded the Stoic school, whose beliefs in a providential deity and in the intrinsic value of virtue were in sharp contrast to Epicurean doctrines. We have no record of Epicurus arguing against the Stoics, but Philodemus' treatise on sign inference shows the Epicureans engaging in extended debate with contemporary Stoics on the basis for empirical generalizations, and Cicero's *On the Nature of the Gods* records their criticisms of Stoic theology. Secondly, there is some dissent within Epicureanism. For instance, Cicero records that some Epicureans thought – against the orthodox line – that friends come to love their friends for their own sake and that not all mental pleasures depend on bodily pleasures.

Non-Epicureans

Reports on Epicureanism are scattered across a huge range of authors, but two are worth special mention. The Roman statesman and philosophical enthusiast Cicero (106–43 BCE) counted himself an adherent of Plato's sceptical Academy. During an enforced hiatus from Roman politics near the end of his life, he decided to serve his countrymen by composing treatises in Latin summarizing the views of the major philosophical schools on various topics, such as the existence and nature of the gods, fate and freedom, and happiness and the virtues. Usually Cicero composed these as dialogues, with the spokesmen of the various schools debating their positions; often he used the handbooks of the schools themselves (in Greek) as sources for his own productions. Despite Cicero's antipathy to Epicurus, which can cause him to present the Epicurean positions unsympathetically, and his occasional misunderstandings of his sources, Cicero is indispensable.

Sextus Empiricus (*c.* second century CE) was a doctor and Pyrrhonian Sceptic. The Pyrrhonists took as their namesake Pyrrho (*c.*365–270 BCE), a compatriot of Epicurus famous for suspending judgement on all things (i.e. having no beliefs) and obtaining peace of mind as a result. But the Pyrrhonian movement was founded by Aenesidemus in the first century BCE, when he thought the sceptical Academy was insufficiently sceptical, and Sextus is our main source of information on it. One of the main Pyrrhonist procedures is to present arguments on various sides of some issue – for instance, the Stoic arguments in favour of divine providence and the Epicurean arguments against it – in such a way that the opposing arguments have "equal weight", with the result that suspension of judgement follows; for example, you do not have a belief one way or the other about the existence of divine providence. Because of this sceptical practice, Sextus presents an impressive array of arguments by various philosophers, including the Epicureans.

There are numerous other sources of information on Epicureanism, of varying reliability, which either summarize parts of its doctrine or preserve short quotations from Epicurus.[3] These sources, all together, allow us to piece together a reasonably complete picture of Epicurus' philosophy. However, gaps and controversies remain.

PART I

Metaphysics and physics: introduction and overview

Epicurus divides philosophy into three parts: physics, "canonic" and ethics (*DL* X 29–30). Canonic deals with the standards used to judge what is the case (which in contemporary philosophy falls under the heading "epistemology"), and ethics with what to pursue, what to avoid and what the goal of human life is. These parts of the system will be explored later in the book.

Epicurean "physics" covers the entire theory of nature (*phusis* in Greek, from which "physics" is derived): what the basic constituents of the natural world are and how one explains the processes within it. So Epicurean "physics" covers much of the same ground as does contemporary physics, for example in its theorizing about the types of atomic motion and how atoms form larger bodies, and in its cosmology. However, it extends considerably further. Since it concerns change in the natural world as a whole, biological questions (such as how one explains the apparent functional organization of creatures' organs) and psychological questions (such as how one accounts for vision) also fall under the purview of Epicurean "physics". Furthermore, Epicurus thinks that the natural world is all that exists, so Epicurean "physics" is really a general theory of what exists and what its nature is. Thus, Epicurean "physics" addresses issues that many (although not all) philosophers would think are more properly metaphysical and not scientific: what the relationship of the mind to the body is and whether there is an afterlife; whether the gods exist and, if they do, what they are like; and whether only material things exist as such. So this section is entitled "metaphysics and physics", although the Epicureans themselves would not have used this terminology.

Epicurus' metaphysics is resolutely materialistic: the only things that exist *per se* are atoms and void. Atoms are uncuttable bits of solid body, moving through void, which is simply empty space. Atoms have a limited stock of properties: size, shape, weight and resistance to blows (Chapter 2). These atoms fall through space because of their weight, and in order to explain how they collide, rebound and become entangled with one another to form macroscopic bodies, Epicurus posits a random atomic swerve (Chapter 3). There are many properties, such as being weary, being red or being a stimulant, that can be possessed only by conglomerates of atoms, not individual atoms, and are thus "emergent" in *some* sense. Yet Epicurus wants to say that only atoms and void exist *per se*, and that the possession of these emergent properties by macroscopic objects can be exhaustively explained in terms of the properties of the atoms that make up these objects, along with their relations to other atoms. In particular, Epicurus wants to account for the reality of sensible qualities, such as redness and bitterness, within his reductionist programme. Democritus denied that such properties really exist, saying that in truth there is only atoms and void, and this leads him to doubt the reliability of the senses; Epicurus needs to combat Democritus on this question (Chapter 4).

One important result of Epicureans physics is that a satisfying explanation for the formation of the world, and for phenomena such as earthquakes and rain, can be given entirely in terms of atomic motions, which he thinks *excludes* explanations that appeal to divine will (Chapter 5). In the biological realm, too, we can account for the functioning of organisms from the "bottom up" in terms of atoms and their properties, without any reference to purposes or functions within nature (Chapter 6). We are among those organisms, and the functioning of our minds is included in this programme: the mind is simply a bodily organ responsible for mental functions such as perception, as the heart is the organ responsible for pumping our blood. An important upshot of this analysis is that death is annihilation (Chapter 7). Such a materialistic view of the world might seem incompatible with human beings having freedom of action, but Epicurus tries to accommodate the possibility of freedom in the world, in part by using the indeterministic atomic "swerve" that somehow allows us to act as we wish (Chapter 8).

TWO

Atoms and void

The existence of atoms and void

There are bodies in motion. No argument is needed to establish this; we simply see bodies in motion. Epicurus may have tossed a rock in the air and pointed at it if asked to demonstrate this point, and if someone pressed him further even after he done this, he may have tossed a rock *at* the person. (In Chapter 9 we shall explore further Epicurus' arguments against the sceptic, and in Chapter 10 his account of the role sensation plays in gaining knowledge of the world.) From this observation, it follows trivially that there are bodies. But establishing the existence of void – where "void" is simply empty space in which there are no bodies – requires some argument. The basic argument, however, is simple (*Ep. Hdt.* 40, *DRN* I 329–45):

1. If there is motion, there is void.
2. There is motion.

---

3. Therefore, there is void.

Premise 2, as indicated above, is supposed to be a datum of experience. As for premise 1, if the universe were a plenum – that is, if it were packed totally full of body, with no empty space – there would be nowhere for bodies to move into, and so they would not move at all. That is because part of what makes bodies what they are is that they resist blows: they do not allow things to move through them; they get in the way. Once there is empty space a body in motion can run into a second body and sometimes push it out of the way, as the second body in turn moves into empty space.

Lucretius gives a second *reductio* argument for the existence of void: if there were no void, all objects of equal size should have equal weight, since, being equally full of body, they would have equal quantities of matter. But this conclusion is obviously false. To account for the fact that a ball of wool weighs much less than a ball of lead of equal diameter, we must suppose that the ball of wool has more void space within it than does the ball of lead (*DRN* I 360–69).

The Epicureans were in a minority in believing in the existence of absolutely empty space, and plenum theorists would not be impressed with either of these arguments. As to the first, plenum theorists had their own explanation of how motion could happen in a plenum, via "reciprocal replacement": the place that a moving body formerly occupied allows the bodies that it is pushing aside somewhere to go. The simplest example of this would be a rotating sphere; each piece of the sphere may push aside an adjacent piece, and each piece will have somewhere to go, without need for any absolutely empty space. Lucretius gives the slightly different example of a fish nosing through water, with the water it displaces going around its sides and filling in the space behind it where it used to be (*DRN* I 370–86). He inadequately objects to this theory by saying that the fish's motion could not start unless there were some space already there for the water to move into, and before the fish begins moving that space is not available.

As to the second, Aristotle thought that heaviness and lightness were irreducible qualities of different types of matter, as opposed to being a function of the quantity of "full" space. Also, Lucretius' argument presupposes that space is either absolutely empty or absolutely full, with "full" space being equal in density. However, the Presocratic Anaximenes (for instance) thought that the fundamental element, air, could exist in various states of density or rarefaction. Dense air forms stones and earth, less dense air water and clouds, and the most rarefied air becomes fire (Simpl. *in Phys.* 24, 26ff. [DK 13 A5]). If one thinks that matter is "squashable" in this way, one could account for differences in weight without positing void. Indeed, squashable matter would allow one to account for motion without void: even if the matter in front of a moving body would have no place to go, the moving body could compact it, while the matter behind the moving body expands to fill the space it formerly occupied.

Others went on the offensive against the intelligibility of void. In fact, the notion of void was not developed originally by Leucippus or Democritus, the inventors of atomism, but by Melissus, an Eleatic. The Eleatics (the more famous of whom were Parmenides and Zeno of Elea) gave arguments against the possibility of plurality and change that were entirely *a priori*, that is, based on logical and not empirical considerations. Melissus argued against the existence of motion as follows (Simpl. *in Phys.* 112, 6 [DK 30 B7]):

1. There is no void.
2. If there is motion, there is void.

---

3. Therefore, there is no motion.

The basic consideration from which many Eleatic arguments begin is the apparently truistic "What is, is, and what is not, is not". Melissus applies this to void. If void is just nothingness, it is "what is not". But to assert the existence of what is not is contradictory. So void does not exist. Since void is a necessary condition on motion, however, it follows that motion does not exist either.

Leucippus and Democritus both argue that there is nothing incoherent about the notion of void. Void is defined privatively: it is where there is not body. And so, in some sense, void is non-being and nothing – that is, it is not a *being*, not a *thing* – but it does not follow that void does not exist at all or lacks all properties. It is simply empty space, and so we can say where it is, and say that as empty space it is yielding, in the sense of allowing bodies to enter into it and giving way with no resistance. Aristotle reports that Leucippus and Democritus were happy to advance the seemingly (but not actually) paradoxical claim that "what is not" exists no less than "what is" (Arist. *Metaph.* I.4 985b4 [DK 67 A4]).

The Epicureans would agree with the above, but they take a different tack: if you think you are having trouble conceiving what void could be, all you need to do is think of the empty space around you right now, through which you could toss a rock if you wished. That is what void is like. The analogy is imperfect, of course, since, unlike void, the "empty" space in rooms is not *absolutely* empty. (This can be shown by waving a fan near your face and feeling the breeze against your skin. You feel the "blow" of the air because the space around you is full of corporeal bodies; if it were a perfect vacuum, you would feel nothing at all.) Although this "empty" space is not really void, you normally do not see the air around you, and it provides little resistance to the solid bodies moving through it, so it provides a good analogue to the microscopic stretches of absolute void. This strategy of using things at the macro-level to provide analogies of what occurs at the micro-level is quite common in Epicureanism.

So much for void: on to atoms. Before giving Epicurus' argument for their existence, let us describe what they are. The Greek word *atomos* is formed from the root *tomos*, from cut or split, plus the so-called "alpha privative", as in words such as "atheist" (one who believes there is no god) or "apathetic" (lacking in feelings). So, if one wanted to translate the Greek word *atomoi* and not simply transliterate it, "uncuttables" would be a good candidate. Ordinary objects, such as coffee cups, can be broken up into smaller parts. This process of division cannot go on indefinitely, however. Eventually one gets down to the smallest units or building blocks of matter, which cannot be broken down or split up, and out of which all compound bodies are composed. These are atoms.

The Epicureans give at least three arguments for the existence of these indivisible bits of body. The first (*Ep. Hdt.* 41, *DRN* I 540–47) is that, if all bodies are liable to be split up, then eventually they would all be reduced to nothingness. And since the universe has existed forever – a point we shall return to later – if this reduction to nothing would eventually happen, it would have happened by now, which is inconsistent with our observations. Unfortunately, it is unclear why an indefinite series of divisions would entirely annihilate things rather than simply produce infinitesimal bits of matter. Later Lucretius makes a slightly different point: if division could continue indefinitely, then over time the bits of matter would be worn down to such a extent that, even if they were to *exist*, they would be unable to produce the complex compound bodies, especially living things, that we observe (*DRN* I 551–64).

The second argument (*DRN* I 526–39) depends on the Epicurean theory of how division occurs. Ordinary compound bodies are made up of smaller pieces that are entangled with one another in various ways, but they also contain void spaces. In such cases, a blow from outside can force the pieces apart and spilt the body. Eventually, however, you will come to a piece that is all "solid" space and no void; imagine a perfectly solid, tiny, cubical hunk of matter. In such a case, a blow from another body would make the hunk of matter as a whole bounce away, but without any void spaces to force sub-pieces apart, it would not fissure.

Finally, the existence of an enduring set of atomic constituents with fixed shapes is needed in order to explain the regularities we observe at the macroscopic level (*DRN* I 584–98). This, in turn, depends on the widely accepted general principle, first explicitly formulated by Parmenides, that nothing comes from nothing. Epicurus says that we must accept that nothing comes to be from what is not, because otherwise everything would come to be from everything (*Ep. Hdt.* 38). This seems not to follow. Luckily, Lucretius gives a more extended discussion of this principle, in which he tries to give it empirical support through the phenomena of biological generation (*DRN* I 159–214). We see that things come to be from certain sources (e.g. pears from pear trees), at certain times (e.g. roses in the spring, grapes in the autumn), in certain places (e.g. fish in the water) and in certain manners (e.g. adulthood following adolescence). But if we were to give up the principle that nothing comes to be from nothing, then *anything* would be able to come to be from *anything*, in any manner whatsoever. Lucretius lists some of the absurdities we might then encounter, such as human beings springing from the sea, and children too young to talk instantly becoming young adults. So the general principle of "nothing from nothing", which Parmenides and many others take to be an *a priori* truth, is given empirical support by the Epicureans.

The Epicureans also accept the corollary principle that nothing perishes into nothing (*Ep. Hdt.* 39, *DRN* I 215–64). If things that were destroyed perished utterly – rather than being resolved into components that could then make new beings – then by now everything would have been annihilated.

We must accept that there is a reason why things occur in the way that they do, and not otherwise. Having a stock of unalterable atomic units of matter allows us to explain the world of orderly change and plurality without violating the Parmenidean sayings. The things we see come into being and pass away. Their ultimate constituents, however, do not *come* into being, but have instead always existed, and will always exist.

The properties of atoms and void

Only bodies and void exist *per se*, that is, exist without depending for their existence on something else. A pocket of void space between the earth and the moon, or the cubical atom as it rebounds from a collision, is ontologically basic. All other things that exist are ultimately explicable as attributes of bodies. Motion exists, but does not exist on its own: there must a body that is moving. Likewise, sizes (like two metres long) exist, but are attributes of some body. And time is a measure of motion, an "accident of an accident". It is a property of motion and other change – there could not be a stretch of time in which absolutely nothing is happening – with motion and other change in turn being attributes of bodies (*Ep. Hdt.* 68–73, Sext. Emp. *Math.* X 219–27).

Some of these attributes are permanent, for example the shape of an atom, while others are temporary, for example my present high caffeine level. We shall look at the properties of compound bodies, such as coffee's being bitter and a stimulant, in Chapter 4. For the moment, let us remain with atoms. Atoms have a very limited stock of properties: size, shape, location, weight and resistance to blows. These properties are simply constitutive of what it is to be a body. Something could not be bodily without being located somewhere and having a shape of some sort, and in order to have a shape it must also be extended. And if a body did not get in the way when another body tried to move into the space it was occupying – if it simply were to give way without resistance – it would not be a corporeal body at all, but simply void, which is incorporeal, that is, non-bodily. In fact, it is this "yielding" that distinguishes void from body, since void space also has size, shape and location.

Epicurus carefully notes that these properties do not exist *per se*, although they certainly exist. He further claims that they are not "parts" of the atom in the same sense in which the wheels and windows are parts of my car. But the body gets its permanent nature *as a body* from all of these properties together. So even though atoms do exist *per se*, it would also be acceptable to think of an atom as being just a complex of size, shape, hardness and so on; that is all there is to being that atom (Sext. Emp. *Math.* X 257). This allows Epicurus to sidestep a problem that John Locke encounters (although obviously he did not devise his doctrine to avoid Locke's difficulties). For Locke, physical substance is the underlying substratum that supports bodily qualities such as size and shape. But the substance considered in itself, apart from the qualities it supports, becomes a mysterious "I know not what" (*Essay Concerning Human Understanding* II 23).

Epicureans assert that atoms do *not* have properties such as colour and odour (*DRN* II 730–1022). The main reason for excluding such properties is that atoms are supposed to be the stable building blocks out of which all other things arise, and that do not change in their intrinsic properties at all, but only in their locations and relationships to one another. Other things come to be and perish, while the atoms always are. However, colours, odours, and the like are all variable: the same sea can turn from dark to white when the wind whips it up, even though the atoms that compose it are mostly the same.

Lucretius adds two points. First, the idea of a colourless body is not incoherent. Just as through touch blind people can form the conception of a body not connected to any colour, so too can we

(*DRN* II 739–48). Lucretius also appeals to the Epicurean theory of how bodies can possess qualities such as odours (which we shall look into later): bodies have sensible qualities because they emit streams of particles that interact with our sense-organs. So a hunk of Limburger cheese smells wonderful because of particles wafting from it that enter our noses. But individual atoms, as indivisible units of matter, cannot emit streams of particles from themselves, and hence cannot themselves have sensible properties (*DRN* II 842–64).

Minimal parts

Atoms are *physically* indivisible, for the reasons given above. However, they are *theoretically* divisible, as they have spatial sub-parts. A cubical atom will have a top and bottom half; in a knobbly atom, each of the knobs would be a distinct (although undetachable) part. The Epicureans, however, think that even this process of *theoretical* division cannot go on indefinitely. Eventually, we would arrive at absolutely smallest spatial units, or spatial minima. All magnitudes are "composed" of a finite number of these spatial minima.

Why think that space is quantized in this way? The Epicureans give two primary arguments (*Ep. Hdt.* 57, *DRN* I 599–634). The first derives from the arguments of Zeno of Elea against motion.[1] Before something can move from A to B, it would have to reach the midpoint of A and B. Call this C. But then, in order to reach C, it would have to reach the midpoint of A and C. Call this D. And so on and so forth: since this process of division can continue infinitely, for an object to move anywhere at all, it will have to move across an infinite number of points. And if it is impossible to pass across an infinite number of things in a finite time (as Zeno believes it is; Arist. *Ph.* 233a21 [DK 29 A25]), then motion is impossible. Epicurus agrees that it is impossible to move across an unlimited number of parts. But instead of accepting the manifestly false conclusion that there is no motion, he simply denies that bodies (or spaces generally) can, even theoretically, be divided without limit. So the path from A to B will contain a finite number of spatial intervals, and Zeno's conclusion is avoided.

The second argument is that any body (or spatial magnitude, more broadly speaking) made up of an infinite number of spatial parts, where those parts are themselves finite in size, would have to be infinite in size. But, obviously, not all bodies are infinite in size.

An obvious objection to Epicurus' doctrine is that the notion of spatial minima is inconceivable. Take any spatial magnitude you wish. No matter how small it is, you can conceive (at least theoretically) of dividing it in half, and hence it is not a minimum. Epicurus anticipates this objection and tries to reply to it by drawing an analogy between spatial and perceptible minima (*Ep. Hdt.* 58–9). In vision, objects can get smaller and smaller, to the point where they can get no smaller without becoming imperceptible. Think of minute dust motes, or a car shrinking as it moves further away, until the last moment in which it can be seen before it vanishes. Such objects will have extension: they must in order to be visible. But they will have no perceptible sub-parts, because any spatial sub-parts would be below our threshold to see them. Such perceptible minima are not literally spatial minima; dust motes are both physically and theoretically divisible. But perceptible minima allow us to conceive of what theoretical spatial minima are like, as extended yet partless, and to answer the objection.

Epicureans draw a number of startling conclusions from this theory (Simpl. *in Phys.* 934, 23–30).[2] Besides space, both motion and time will have minima. The smallest amount one can move is by one spatial unit. Think of a video character moving across a pixellated screen, one pixel at a time. It cannot move half a pixel. And because time is a measure of motion, there will also be temporal "atoms": the interval of a body moving one spatial minimum. Time and motion both will be "jerky", then: a series of snapshots, like the stills making up a film reel, of bodies moving on a pixellated background.

This theory also allows the Epicureans to declare a universal speed limit. Assuming that bodies cannot "skip" spatial minima when moving, then the fastest speed would be going from A to B in a number of temporal "atoms" equal to the number of spatial minima from A to B, that is, making the trip entirely unimpeded.

The doctrine of spatial minima also raises interesting problems for geometry. For instance, the Pythagoreans had already demonstrated that certain magnitudes, such as the length of a side of a square and of its diagonal, are incommensurable. But if magnitudes are composed of a whole number of spatial minima, it follows that all magnitudes are commensurable with one another. Too bad for geometry, conclude the Epicureans. Cicero relates the story of a follower of Epicurus, Polyaenus (*Academica* II 106), who started as a mathematician but, after converting to Epicureanism, became convinced that all of geometry was false.[3]

Conclusion

To account for a world of bodies in motion, there must be void, and to account for the order and stability we see around us, there must be a changeless stock of uncuttable basic particles out of which all of the bodies we perceive are composed. These basic particles possess only a Spartan set of qualities. The Epicureans believe, over-optimistically, that only this view of the world is consistent with the phenomena. In any case, having now (purportedly) established the basic principle of their physics on the basis of observation, the task of going back up to the phenomena and adequately explaining them via their physics still lies open. Before we follow them there, however, let us briefly linger at the level of atoms and the causes of their motion.

THREE
Atomic motion

Weight and the swerve

Up to this point, Epicurus' atomism has largely followed the path already taken by Democritus. Since we have fairly little information about Democritus, it is possible that some of the particular arguments that Epicurus and Lucretius give for the existence of atoms are original, but the basic argument that void is necessary for there to be motion, and the characterization of atoms and void, are more or less the same.

But when accounting for atomic motion, Epicurus makes major modifications to the system he inherited from Democritus. For Democritus, atoms eternally fly through the void in all directions. They collide with and rebound from one another, occasionally becoming entangled and forming larger bodies. Atomic motion, then, is the result of inertia – although one must always be careful of anachronism when applying such terms – plus collisions.

Epicurus adds two additional causes of atomic motion. The first is weight (*DRN* II 184–215). For Epicurus, "weight" is simply the natural tendency of atoms to move downwards.[1] What way is "down"? If you stand upright (no leaning!) and draw a line from the top of your head down to your feet, it is that way, below you, whereas "up" is the opposite direction. Epicurus (like Democritus) believes that the universe is spatially unlimited (we shall explore the reasons for this in Chapter 5). So one can go downwards forever; imagine following the *y*-axis in a Cartesian coordinate grid from 0, through –1 and –2 and so on, indefinitely. So, *contra* Aristotle (*Ph.* IV 8, 215a6–10), we can make perfectly good sense of the notion of "down" without the notion of a lowest point or bottom.

If unimpeded, atoms naturally fall downwards at equal speed, that is, at maximum speed, one spatial minimum per temporal minimum. Larger, heavier atoms do not travel faster than smaller ones. Instead, the reason why we experience that heavier bodies normally fall faster than lighter ones is that they are better able to push aside the impediments offered by air or water (*Ep. Hdt.* 61, *DRN* II 225–42).

But this raises a problem. As Lucretius puts it, if the only natural motion of atoms was to fall straight downwards at equal speeds, then the atoms would all "fall downwards, like drops of rain, through the deep void, and neither would a collision occur, nor a blow be produced among the primary bodies: in this way nature would have never produced anything" (*DRN* II 221–4, trans. Smith).

This leads to the second additional cause of atomic motion: the swerve. At "uncertain times and places" (*DRN* II 218–19) atoms swerve to the side by one spatial minimum. This additional cause of atomic motion is needed for the atoms ever to have collided and produced the bodies we see: without the swerve, the atoms would be like cars being driven along a multi-lane highway at equal speed, staying in their lanes. An occasional swerve to the side, however, is enough not only to cause a collision, but to start a chain reaction of additional collisions as a result of the blow started by the sideways swerve. (This may be dubbed the "cosmogonic" argument for the swerve, as the swerve is supposed to be needed for the creation for all macroscopic bodies and *a fortiori* our *cosmos*. More famously, the indeterminate atomic swerve is supposed to be needed to preserve our freedom from the "decrees of fate". We shall look at that role of the swerve in Chapter 8.)

The basic form of Lucretius' cosmogonic argument is the same as that for the existence of void. We start from something evident in our experience (that there is motion, that there are macroscopic bodies), and on its basis we infer a conclusion about what is not in itself directly observable (the existence of absolutely empty space, or of tiny atomic swerves). It goes as follows:

1. If the atoms did not swerve, there would be no collisions and no macroscopic bodies.
2. There are collisions and macroscopic bodies.

---

3. Thus, the atoms swerve.

The crucial premise, of course, is the first. A natural way of reading this "cosmogonic" argument is parallel to *kalam*-type cosmological arguments for God's existence advanced by Islamic thinkers who think the world must have some temporal starting-point: given that there are collisions, there must be some first collision in order to get the sequence of collisions started.[2] And given the Epicurean theory of the natural downwards motion of atoms at a uniform velocity, the only way for the sequence of collisions to get started is for the atoms (or at least one atom) to depart from their usual motion and to bump into neighbouring atoms.

But on this interpretation, the argument is pitifully deficient. It suffers from two crippling problems, one philosophical, the other textual. The philosophical problem is that there is no reason for the Epicureans to suppose that there needs to be an initial collision to get collisions started. Instead, one can simply suppose that there is an infinite series of collisions extending backwards in time. Any particular collision is caused by the velocities and directions of motion of the atoms that collide, which in turn are caused (in part) by the past collisions of those atoms, and so on, on down the line. And indeed, this is precisely the theory advanced by Democritus. Since there is already an economical explanation of collisions available, adding the swerve would be gratuitous.

The textual problem is that the Epicureans explicitly deny that there ever was an initial atomic collision to get things started. The universe (i.e. the totality of atoms and void) has existed forever, since there is nothing else that exists from which it could come into existence (*Ep. Hdt.* 39), and nothing comes into being from nothing.

More crucially, atomic collisions have been going on forever. Epicurus describes the different sorts of atomic motions: he asserts that atoms are constantly moving, with some atoms separated far from others in solitary motion, while others are tangled together, but even these are vibrating back and forth as they collide with one another. He then adds that there is no beginning to these sorts of motions, since the atoms and void are eternal (*Ep. Hdt.* 43–4). Likewise, Lucretius says that generation and destruction have always existed (*DRN* II 569–80), and that every possible combination of atoms has already come into existence, since the atoms have always been driven by collisions and their weight (*DRN* V 187–91).

Since postulating the swerve to give a temporal start to collisions (a) is gratuitous and (b) contradicts what the Epicureans say elsewhere, we have strong grounds on the principle of charity to seek a different interpretation of the argument.[3] (Basically, the principle of charity is a methodological principle on how to interpret texts or speech, in which you give the person the benefit of the doubt and presume that what is being said is reasonable. So if a person appears to be saying something incoherent, utterly unjustified or incredibly obtuse, instead of jumping all over the person for his failures, you should step back and consider whether you have misunderstood what is being said, and try to find a plausible way of understanding it so that it is not so bad.)

Aristotle's criticisms of Democritus

Since Epicurus probably added weight and the swerve as causes of atomic motion in order to overcome difficulties of Democritus' theory, a promising place to look for some problems would be previous criticisms of that theory. The most extensive such criticisms were by Aristotle.

Aristotle's criticisms of Democritus are largely based on the distinction between natural and forced motion. For Aristotle, natural motion is caused by an individual's own nature: an internal source of change. For instance, earth is by nature heavy, and it naturally falls down (where "down", for Aristotle, is towards the centre of the cosmos, the goal of its downwards motion). But sometimes this natural motion can be impeded, and something will engage in forced motion; for example, if I cruelly hoist a clod of earth up in the air in order to prevent it from fulfilling its goal, the upwards motion of the earth caused by my intervention is forced. According to Aristotle, all atomic motion is forced, since all motions are simply the result of blows by other atoms, and no atomic motion is natural, since atoms have no natural direction of motion. Aristotle thinks that the absence of natural motion makes any motion whatsoever impossible (*Ph.* IV 8, 215a1–13; *Cael.* III 2, 300b9–16).

Democritus would seem to have a ready reply available (if he were around at the time): why should he accept Aristotle's presupposition that there must be some natural motion in order for there to be motion at all, as opposed to simply conceding (using Aristotle's vocabulary) that all motion is forced? After all, each "forced" motion has an explanation for why it occurs because of some previous "forced" motion, which in turn was the result of other past "forced" motions, and so on.

Aristotle, however, would not be satisfied by this reply. Aristotle is not looking for an explanation of any *particular* motion in terms of past motions, but for why there should be motion at all, and he sees no explanations forthcoming from Democritus. Simply saying that there has always been movement, as the early atomists do, is not sufficient to explain why movement occurs at all, and why it occurs in the way it does (*Metaph.* XII 6 1071b31–4; *Ph.* VIII 1 252a32–b2). Aristotle points out that there is nothing about the nature either of the atoms or of the void that *explains* why the atoms move rather than eternally sit still, since the atoms have no natural motion, and void does not move the atoms either, but simply gives space for things to move through.

Weight and the swerve as responses to Aristotle

Atomic weight gives Epicurus a reply to Aristotle. There are other decent grounds for positing the existence of a natural tendency for bodies to fall downwards: our daily experience makes it evident that bodies have weight, which gives them a natural motion "down". (*Ep. Hdt.* 60 suggests this.) But weight also gives an explanation for why the atoms move at all rather than simply sitting still. Epicurus accepts Aristotle's thesis that there must be some natural motion in order for there to be motion. A later report attributes to him the view that atoms would not move at all if they were not moved by their weight (Aëtius I.3.18ff., IG I-77). Weight does not *start* the atoms moving; instead, it explains why they have been moving eternally.

The swerve can fulfil a similar role, explaining why there are atomic collisions and the compound bodies that result from atomic collisions. If the only natural motion of the atoms were straight down, we *would* expect that the atoms *would* fall straight downwards, like drops of rain in the night, never touching. There would be no satisfactory explanation in terms of the properties of the atoms – their extension, solidity or weight – for why there are collisions at all. Once there is a swerve, however, we can appeal to a natural feature of atomic motion to account for the existence of collisions. The swerve does not get collisions *started*; instead, it explains why atoms have been eternally colliding.

This makes the introduction of the swerves more understandable, but the argument still suffers from at least two problems. The first stems from the swerves' second function: to break the decrees of fate. The swerves happen at uncertain times and places. And because this uncertainty is supposed to prevent new atomic movements from being invariably linked to old ones, which is needed to preserve our freedom, Lucretius is not saying merely that we cannot *know* when swerves will occur. His point is metaphysical, not epistemic: there is nothing in the natures of the atoms or their past motions that determines where and when swerves will occur; they are genuinely indeterministic. Critics of Epicurus scorned this as introducing "motion without a cause" (e.g. Cic. *Fat.* 22–5). But if swerves have no cause, then introducing them does not help to explain why collisions occur. Epicurus would have been better off simply admitting that collisions have always been occurring. At least then there would be an explanation why the individual collisions occur, in terms of past collisions. Trying to explain the existence of collisions by introducing causeless atomic swerves, which are *entirely* inexplicable, just makes things worse.

This problem can be overcome. Atoms have a natural tendency to swerve occasionally to the side in an indeterministic manner, just as they have a natural tendency to fall straight downwards. So, an atom's falling downwards has a cause: the latter natural tendency of the atom, which we call "weight". Likewise, an atom's swerving to the side has a cause: the former natural tendency of the atom. If we wish, we could call this atomic property "swerviness". So swerves do have an atomic cause (swerviness), even though the particular time and place in which swerves occur is not causally necessitated. By its nature, swerviness operates erratically.[4]

The second problem is that the swerve is *ad hoc*. It gets around the difficulty at hand, but it is cheap and arbitrary. It is not very satisfactory simply to assert that atoms have an inherent tendency to swerve off to the side every once in a while and hit one another after one has realized that they would never collide if they all naturally fell downwards at equal speed.

Conclusion

Epicurus has three principles to explain atomic motion – weight, the swerve and collisions – whereas Democritus has only one, collisions. These additional principles, and the arguments for them, are problematic. Still, they show Epicurus' willingness to modify even the fundamental principles of Democritean atomism in order to overcome its perceived shortcomings. For Epicurus, events in the world are supposed ultimately to be explained by appealing to atoms and atomic properties, but under the Democritean physics there is no good explanation for the motion of the atoms. Democritus can account for each individual motion, but not for why motion exists at all, or for the particular types of motion that one encounters. Epicurus' modifications help to remedy this deficiency. The natural downwards motion accounts for the existence of motion, while the swerve accounts for the existence of collisions and compound bodies.

FOUR

Sensible qualities

While Epicurus does make significant changes to Democritean atomism by adding weight and the swerve as causes of atomic motion, his ontology at the level of atoms is basically the same: the ultimate constituents of the universe are void, which is simply empty space, and atoms, which are extended bits of matter, eternal and changeless except in their locations. We infer that these entities exist on the basis of our perception of a world of changeable, temporary objects, objects that, unlike the atoms, have properties such as being sweet, hot and red.[1]

Democritus, however, famously denies that these sorts of properties exist in objects. Orange juice may appear to be sweet, but in reality it is no more sweet than it is sour. So our senses systemically mislead us, representing objects as having properties they do not really have, and this makes knowledge difficult, if not impossible, to attain. Epicurus believes that these conclusions are unacceptable, in part because this scepticism would have devastating practical consequences. He needs to reaffirm the reality of these sensible qualities, even while accepting Democritus' basic atomist ontology and theory of perception.

Democritus and the unreality of sensible qualities

After establishing that atoms and void exist, Democritus gives a detailed account of how the perceptual qualities associated with each sense arise as a result of the causal interaction of atoms with the sense-organs.[2] For instance, the taste "bitter" is explained as a result of sharp atoms tearing the tissue of the tongue, "sweet" as the soothing action of round and fairly large atoms on the tongue.[3] The Epicureans largely accept Democritus' account.[4]

However, the same object can affect different percipients differently. The same orange juice that seems pleasingly sweet to most of us will taste unspeakably vile to a person who has just brushed his teeth. A can of soda that looks red to me will have no colour in the dark, and will seem yellow to a dog, as it lacks the retinal cones needed to see red. On the basis of this sort of perceptual relativity, Democritus infers that objects are "no more" (*ou mallon*) sweet than disgusting, no more red than yellow, because they are neither sweet nor disgusting, neither red nor yellow (Sext. Emp. *Pyr.* I 213).

Some properties of bodies *can* be identified with properties of atoms, such as weight and hardness, and these are thought of as real properties of bodies (Theophr. *Sens.* 62). But when we look at the bodies themselves, we discover that, in themselves, the bodies have nothing like "sweetness" or "bitterness" or "redness" in them. Instead, they are simply atomic aggregates that can appear differently to different percipients. Democritus concludes that none of the sensible qualities exist in nature; instead, they are simply affections of the senses (Theophr. *Sens.* 63–4). Sweetness is not out there in the world; it exists only in my mind. This leads to one of Democritus' most famous sayings: "Sweet exists by convention, bitter by convention, colour by convention; atoms and void [alone] exist in reality" and this in turn leads to scepticism: "We know nothing accurately in reality, but only as it changes according to the bodily condition, and the constitution of those things that flow upon (the body) and impinge upon it" (Sext. Emp. *Math.* VII, 135 [DK 68 B9]).

There is a radical discontinuity between the properties to which we have access, and which must form the basis of all our knowledge, and the properties that exist in reality. Democritus says we are severed from reality (Sext. Emp. *Math.* VII, 137 [DK 68 B6]), and he probably has in mind that the sensible qualities, which must form the basis of all knowledge, are found not to be a part of reality, that is, they are merely subjective. In fact, almost all of the reports furnished by the senses (for instance, "The honey is sweet") turn out on inspection to be false. We *think* that the honey itself is really sweet, but the sweetness is not in the honey at all: it is simply a change in our sense-organ. Democritus' epistemological pessimism is widely reported; for instance, he says that we know nothing, because truth is in an abyss (*DL* VII 72 [DK 68 B117]), and that we do not grasp how each thing is or is not.

The complaint of the senses against reason shows that Democritus is well aware of the possibly self-stultifying nature of his philosophy: "Wretched mind, do you take your evidence from us and then try to overthrow us? Our overthrow is your downfall" (reported in Gal. *On Medical Experience* XV 8 [DK 68 B125], trans. Hankinson 1995). There is a painful irony in Democritus' philosophy: his atomism is a response to the Eleatic philosophers, such as Parmenides and Melissus, who deny the reality of change and the phenomenal world. Atomism is supposed to provide an answer to the Eleatic challenge, as well as provide economical and comprehensive causal explanations for the features of the world. Democritus' atomism, however, undercuts the authority of the senses as a source of information about the world, which in turn leads to the collapse of reason, including the theories arrived at by the use of reason, such as atomism.[5]

Epicurus and the reality of the relational

The Epicureans believe that Democritus' doctrines lead to full-blown scepticism and make life impossible: saying that every single thing is "no more this than that", for example no more sweet than bitter, throws our life into chaos (Plut. *Adv. Col.* 1108f). Epicurus tries to avoid this scepticism, and its devastating practical consequences, by staunchly defending the reality of sensible qualities. He denies the validity of Democritus' inference of the unreality of sensible qualities on the basis of perceptual relativity, and he does so as part of a wide-ranging defence of the reality of the relative.

Democritus is far from the only figure to deploy an *ou mallon* (no more) argument. For instance, the sophist Protagoras says that the wind is, in itself, no more hot than cold, because it is *both* hot and cold. He avoids contradiction by saying that it is hot for one person, and it is cold for another (Pl. *Tht.* 152b). Plato is no sceptic, but he often uses *ou mallon* arguments to show that some property cannot be truly instantiated in the phenomenal world. Plato frequently employs the principle that for any thing to be truly *F*, it must be *F* without qualification. So, for instance, for something to be truly just, it must be always just, not just at some times and unjust at others. Or, to use another example, Socrates says that a beautiful maiden is not truly beautiful because, although she is beautiful in comparison to monkeys, she is not beautiful in comparison to the gods (Pl. *Hp. mai.* 289b–d). Later sceptics have an epistemological reading of the *ou mallon* principle. They start from the fact of the relativity of perceptual qualities, or of value predicates, and argue that we can no more say that the thing is *F* than not-*F*, because we have no criterion by which to judge between the reports and decide which property the object itself has (Sext. Emp. *Pyr.* I 188).

Despite this great diversity among the different uses of the *ou mallon* argument, all of those who use the argument have a common interest in what a thing is "by nature" (*phusis*). And what this seems to mean, generally, is what a thing is in and of itself, that is, what it is intrinsically. The theme that is consistent throughout the various *ou mallon* arguments is the move from the observation that some property of an object differs relative to different observers, times or conditions (*a* appears *F* to me but not-*F* to you, or is *F* under certain circumstances but not-*F* under others) to the conclusion either that the object does not, in itself, have that property, or that we cannot know whether the object has that property or not.

The Epicureans, however, admit relational and dispositional properties into their ontology. Lucretius includes servitude, liberty and poverty among his list of accidental properties (*DRN* I 455–6). If "servitude" is a real property in one's ontology, it cannot be an *intrinsic* property, because a person is not enslaved *per se*, but only because of certain very complex relationships that hold between him and other people.

The Epicureans believe that a correct understanding of the nature of relational properties defeats sceptical *ou mallon* arguments. Polystratus, the third head of Epicurus' Garden, makes a sustained and convincing defence of the reality of relational and dispositional predicates, in the course of defending the reality of value properties "fair" and "foul" against the charge that these things are falsely believed in, because what is fair and foul is not the same everywhere and under all circumstances (Polystratus *On Irrational Contempt* 23.26–26.23, LS 7D). He says that relative predicates do not have the same status as things said not relatively, so we should not expect them to behave in the same way. For example, "bigger" is a relational predicate, so something cannot be bigger *per se*; it can only be bigger *than something else*. So to say that Simmias is not "really" bigger than Socrates because he is both bigger than Socrates but smaller than Phaedo would be naive.

Polystratus writes that *powers* are the most evident case of such relational properties. It is not the case that the same things are nourishing or deadly for all creatures; instead, the same thing can be nourishing for some but deadly for others. But we do not conclude on this basis that properties such as deadliness are nonexistent. Peanuts may be deadly for somebody with an allergy but nourishing for other people, and cyanide may be deadly poison for me and not poisonous for some race of aliens. But that does not make cyanide "no more deadly than not deadly", so that I become sceptical about the deadliness of cyanide *for me*. If I really think so, I should swallow some and see what happens, thus incrementally reducing the number of sceptics in the world. The deadliness of the cyanide for me is a real property, albeit a relational one, *of the cyanide*, not something that is merely conventional or subjective. And this is exactly what we should expect, if we understand the sort of property deadliness should be.

The Epicureans seem to think that the sensible qualities of bodies are such dispositional qualities. In discussing the properties of wine,

Epicurus says that it would be a mistake to think that wine generally has heating or cooling properties. Instead, it has a mixture of powers, such that a certain quantity of it would be heating for certain individuals with a certain bodily condition and cooling for others under different circumstances. And he says that the same sort of thing applies to colours: colours are not intrinsic properties but are produced by the ordering and positioning of the atoms in relation to our sight (Plut. *Adv. Col.* 1109e–1110d).

So, it seems, Epicurus thinks that sensible qualities are complicated dispositional properties that cause certain sensory affections within the percipient's mind when interacting with the percipient's sense-organs under certain conditions. This theory would allow Epicurus to admit the phenomena of sensory variability and retain the basic Democritean account of how sensations arise as a result of the interaction of atoms emitted from objects with our sense-organs, while still holding that sensible qualities are real properties of bodies. The can really is red, because it has an atomic make-up such as to cause us to see red under ordinary circumstances. It might not appear red to a dog, but then there is no reason to expect a red object to appear the same way to a dog as it does to us.

Plutarch contends that the Epicurean theory falls prey to the same sort of sceptical difficulties that afflict Democritus. Plutarch notes that Colotes' main objection against Democritus is that Democritus says bodies are in reality "no more this than that". Plutarch says that Epicurus himself, however, admits the relativity of perceptual properties in a way that undermines his claim that they are real properties of objects. Plutarch gives several examples, such as the heating and cooling powers of wine discussed above, and also the way that an object in a dim room may appear coloured to one person and not coloured to another, owing to a difference in the strength of their vision. It follows, thinks Plutarch, that for Epicurus too the can is "no more this way than that", but Epicurus, unlike Democritus, brazenly refuses to admit this consequence of his theory.

Plutarch's objection to Epicurus, however, has little force. It rests on the fact, which Epicurus happily concedes, that the same object, in the same conditions, can appear differently to different percipients. Plutarch concludes from this that sensible qualities are not real properties of objects for Epicurus. This would follow only if, for something to be a *real* property of an object, it must be an *intrinsic* property. But Polystratus explicitly denies this. It is important not to conflate two very different pairs of distinctions: intrinsic versus relative, on the one hand, and objective versus subjective, on the other. The fact that some property is *relative* does not make it thereby *subjective*. Cyanide is deadly *to me*, although maybe not to all organisms. Similarly, the object in the room *really has* the property of causing certain sensations in certain people under certain conditions.

Regarding sensible qualities as dispositional properties does not resolve all possible sceptical difficulties that might arise from the relativity of perception. The same atomic state can cause differing perceptual states, depending on the condition of the percipient. More importantly, the same perceptual state can be caused by differing atomic states. Since this is so, there may be a problem with drawing inferences from perceptual experience about the extra-mental properties of bodies.

This problem may seem to be made even more pressing once we add to the mix the Epicurean doctrine that "all sensations are true". The redness of the can, according to Epicurus, is a real property that the can itself has, in virtue of which it causes people like me to have visual experiences of red. Fair enough. And then, when I see the red can and say "The can is red", I am saying something true. But the perception of the can as yellow by somebody with jaundice is equally true, as is the perception of it as grey by a person with complete colour blindness.

Consideration of these problems will be postponed until Chapter 10. The Epicurean understanding of sensible qualities as dispositional properties does not solve all possible sceptical difficulties. However, it does get around Democritus' worry that because sensible qualities are relative they are somehow not real properties of bodies, but merely subjective.

Furthermore, experiences of bitterness, redness and so on are not caused *merely* by bodies having the dispositional properties to cause such states, although it is true that they do. They have these dispositional properties in virtue of other complicated structural properties of the atoms and groups of atoms; for example, the taste bitter is caused by rough and hooked atoms tearing up the tongue; the various colours we see are caused by the arrangement and shape of the atoms on the surfaces of bodies (scholion to *Ep. Hdt.* 44). Thus, these dispositional properties are tied systematically to complex structural properties of the atoms themselves and the bodies that are constituted by the atoms. This is probably why the atomists often identify having a sensible quality straightforwardly with some atomic property: if the sensible quality is a dispositional quality, and the dispositional property can be explained entirely in terms of some set of atomic properties, it is not difficult to see why the sensible quality would be identified with the atomic property. So the information we receive via sensible qualities is not trivial, because the different sensible qualities are tied to the underlying atomic structures of bodies.

FIVE

Cosmology

The Epicureans try to account for the formation of the earth and of the other heavenly bodies in terms of atoms blindly colliding in the void. Against most other cosmologists, they maintain that our world is only one of an infinite number of worlds, coming to be and falling apart in a spatially infinite universe that has existed and will exist forever. For the Epicureans, however, the most important feature of their cosmology is not that the universe is infinite; it is that it is *purposeless*. Explanations of the formation of the world and of phenomena such as earthquakes and lightning in terms of the interactions of atoms are supposed to displace retrograde and superstitious explanations that appeal to the gods. Not only that: the Epicureans are among the first philosophers to raise the problem of evil in order to argue that the world is not under the control of beneficent gods, as it is too flawed.

The infinite universe

The *cosmos* is our particular ordered world-system: the earth, sun, moon, planets, and stars. Leaving aside the stars – which are thought by the ancient Greeks to be in approximately the same area as the other celestial bodies – the *cosmos* is thus something like the solar system. But there is a sharp divide in antiquity between "two pictures of the world".[1] The first picture, defended by Plato, Aristotle and the Stoics, identifies the *cosmos* and *to pan*, "the all", that is, the physical universe. So on this picture, the universe is finite and unique. Epicurus defends the alternative picture of the world, first developed by Leucippus and Democritus, of an infinite universe. Our particular limited *cosmos* is only one of an infinite number of *cosmoi* (the plural of *cosmos*), each of which comes into existence and will eventually fall apart. But the universe as a whole has no beginning and no end; it has always existed and will always exist. And spatially, the universe stretches infinitely in all directions.

According to the Epicureans, *cosmoi* form when there happens to be a great concentration of matter in one region of space. The *cosmos* starts as a turbulent mass, and the elements of earth, water, air and fiery ether are all mixed together. But over time they begin to separate out, with like element starting to unite with like. But this is not because of any mysterious affinity of like for like. Instead, the particles of earth, as the heaviest element, settled towards the middle of the *cosmos*, squeezing out the lighter elements. So eventually we get layers of earth, then water, then air, then ether. The sun and moon are spherical bodies midway between earth and ether in their density, and they thus float in the air. The settling process does not result in perfect uniformity, however, so some areas of the earth still stick out above the water, and there are high mountains and low plains (*DRN* V 416–508; see also Aëtius 1.4.1–4, IG I-92).

All atoms naturally fall "downwards" at uniform speed, as we have seen (Chapter 3), so "heavier" and "lighter" here do not mean differences in natural rate of fall; instead, "heavier" elements, owing to their size and shape, are better suited to push their way down through "lighter" elements. The "lighter" elements, in turn, are forced upwards by being squeezed that way, even though – *contra* Aristotle – the natural motion of elements such as fire is still down, not up (*DRN* II 184–215).

Our *cosmos* is spherical, as we can see by looking at the dome of the sky, although *cosmoi* come in various shapes (scholion to *Ep. Hdt.* 74). The earth rests on a cushion of air beneath it (scholion to

Ep. Hdt. 73, *DRN* V 534–63). This doctrine raises troubling questions, such as why this portion of air did not get forced upwards in the settling process, and what (if anything) this cushion of air itself rests on. The Epicureans also believe, strangely, that the sun, moon and other celestial bodies are "just as big as they appear to be", unlike most other bodies, which appear smaller than they are as they get further away (*DRN* V 564–73, *Ep. Pyth.* 91). The upshot of this is that these bodies are much smaller than most cosmologists believe they are, although what it means for a body to be just as big as it appears to be, apart from any estimate of how far away it is, is unclear.

In any case, the *cosmos*, like every finite compound body, has come into existence and will eventually fall apart (*Ep. Hdt.* 73, *DRN* V 351–63). But the universe as a whole has no beginning and no end, being simply the totality of atoms moving in the void. As we have seen before (Ch. 2, § "The existence of atoms and void"), the Epicureans accept Parmenides' contention that nothing comes into being from nothing, and so the universe as a whole must always have existed. Likewise, nothing perishes into nothing; instead, compound bodies are resolved into their constituent atoms.

Furthermore, the universe is unlimited spatially. Epicurus says that what is limited has an extreme, an edge. For example, my car is spatially limited, and it has an outer boundary. But an extreme is seen in contrast with something else; that is, there is the edge, and then there is what is beyond the edge. But if that is right, the totality cannot have an edge, since there would then, absurdly, be something in addition to "the all". Hence, the totality of things has no limit (*Ep. Hdt.* 41; see also Simpl. *in Phys.* 203b15 [IG I-90] and *DRN* I 958–67).

Lucretius gives a further argument in support of a spatially unlimited universe (*DRN* I 968–83). (It was originally developed by Archytas of Tarentum, active around Plato's lifetime.) Suppose, for the sake of argument, that there *is* an "edge" to space. Then I could run to that edge and throw a spear. Either the spear will fly past the point at which I launch it, or it will not. If it does, then the supposed "edge" was not really the edge. But if it does not, then something was there to stop the spear from flying onwards, and the supposed "edge" was not really the edge (as the barrier stopping the spear was beyond it). So there cannot be any edge to the universe.

This argument presupposes a Euclidean geometry. It would be grossly unfair to fault the Epicureans on this assumption, as non-Euclidean geometries were not developed until the nineteenth century. Still, it is worth pointing out. On a three-dimensional elliptic geometry, it is possible for a trajectory to continue indefinitely without reaching an edge, even though space is limited. The easiest way to visualize this is to think of the analogous geometry of the surface of a sphere, which is a two-dimensional non-Euclidean geometry. The area of a sphere's surface is limited, even though it has no edge, and you could continue travelling indefinitely along the surface of the sphere (eventually arriving back where you started, if your path is a great circle).

If we leave aside this anachronistic objection, Lucretius' argument seems strong. Lucretius points out that the supposed "edge" of the universe would have to be bounded by empty space, that is, void, which is *something*, although not a "thing". Nonetheless, if he were to hear Lucretius' argument Aristotle would deny this point. Aristotle believes in a unique, spherical, spatially limited *cosmos*, with the earth at the centre and the stars rotating around the centre of the *cosmos* in the outermost heavenly sphere.[2] He would say that, beyond the edge of the *cosmos*, there is literally nothing at all, not even empty space.

That is because, for Aristotle, the fundamental "location" concept is not *space*, but *place*. Aristotle defines the place of some body as "the innermost motionless boundary of what contains it" (*Ph.* IV 4 212a21). If I am sitting in a boat, then the boat would be my "place" in a rough and ready sense, but, strictly speaking, my place is the boundary at the surface of my body, so that nothing is between me and my place. So place exists, but it depends for its existence on the existence of body, because place is just the motionless boundary of some body, which gives it its location. (Place is the *motionless* boundary of a body because moving bodies change their place, while they carry their surfaces with them, and one body can occupy the place previously occupied by another body.) So the idea of there being "place" that is not the place *of* some thing would be rejected by Aristotle; as he puts it, every place has a body in it (*Ph.* IV 1 209a26). Saying that there is a place with no body would be like saying that there is a stretch of time in which no change whatsoever occurred.

If space is infinite, as the Epicureans argue, then there must be an infinite number of atoms and an infinite amount of void. If the number of atoms were limited, they would scatter through the void and not form the bodies as we see them (the effective "density" of atoms would be zero), and if the amount of void were limited (and the effective density of atoms 1), there would not be enough void to allow atoms to move (*Ep. Hdt.* 41–2). And with an infinite number of atoms moving through a limitless void during an infinite stretch of time, there will be an infinite number of *cosmoi* (*Ep. Hdt.* 45). Lucretius adds that there must be life on some of these other worlds, including intelligent life (*DRN* II 1048–1104).

The purposeless universe

The *cosmos* formed simply because of a sorting process of "like to like" when a large number of atoms are congregated together. The Epicureans think that being able to give a non-purposive explanation of the formation of the *cosmos* in this way *excludes* intentional explanations. As Lucretius puts it, the atoms did not get together and make any agreement with one another about how to form the *cosmos*; individual atoms are not the sorts of things that can think. Instead, they fortuitously happened to form it because of "blind" factors such as their weight and shape. And this exclusion of purpose applies also to meteorological phenomena within the *cosmos*, such as eclipses, lightning bolts and earthquakes (*Ep. Hdt.* 76).

Let us suppose that a lightning bolt strikes the hillside above my sister, and a large tree falls down and crushes her to death. I might wail, "Why? *Why* did she die?" The Epicureans would reply that some clouds above my sister collided and struck out numerous seeds of fire, analogous to the way in which two stones or a stone and a chunk of iron strike one another and make sparks (*DRN* VI 160–218). This bolt of fire was strong enough to make a tree fall, and the force of the tree falling on her was enough to crush her, with the resulting shock and loss of blood causing her death. So that is why my sister died. I might not be satisfied with this sort of answer. But the Epicureans would reply that there was no further "reason why" my sister died of the sort I am looking for: no purpose or plan behind the death. It was not punishment for her (or my) sins; it was not meant to teach me a lesson about the transience of life, or anything else like that.

The Epicureans wish to exclude divine agency from the workings of the natural universe. They have an eminently practical reason to do so: a belief in meddling gods is one of the main causes of fear and misery in human life, so to achieve happiness we need to eliminate it. In the opening to book one of *De Rerum Natura*, Lucretius offers a blistering indictment of the evil of superstition and the need for correct philosophy to overcome this evil. Human life was grovelling in the dust, crushed beneath the weight of superstition, until Epicurus discovered the truth about what could be and what could not, and with this knowledge cast down and trampled superstition underfoot and raised us to the heavens in victory (*DRN* I 62–79). Lucretius concludes a long and heartrending description of Agamemnon sacrificing his own daughter in order to appease the gods and gain good winds for sailing off to the Trojan War (*DRN* I 80–101) with the famous line "Such evil deeds can superstition prompt!" (*tantum religio potuit suadere malorum*).

The opponents of the Epicureans – those who wish to attribute natural phenomena to divine agency – can be divided into three camps, camps that may overlap. The first camp contains those who think that heavenly bodies or the *cosmos* as a whole are living beings. Plato, for example, says that the *cosmos* is an animal with a soul (*Ti.* 30b), and the Stoics say god is an immortal animal identical with the world (Plut. *St. Rep.* 1052c–d, LS 46E). And viewing the celestial bodies as divine is widespread in Greek popular religion. The Epicureans have a simple argument against such immanent cosmic deities. Just as fish cannot live in fields, or sap cannot grow in stones, minds cannot exist within any and all sorts of bodies. Minds exist in living creatures; as we shall see, the Epicureans think that they exist in the chests of creatures. But in any case, clods of earth, balls of fire and seas of water cannot have minds, because they are not even alive (*DRN* V 110–45).

The second camp contains those who view the *cosmos* as an artefact, created by a beneficent god. Famously, the Epicureans raise the problem of evil in order to argue against this position. Nowadays, the so-called "logical problem of evil" is often formulated as an alleged inconsistency between the existence of evil, for example the Holocaust, natural disasters and birth defects such as anencephaly, and of an omnipotent (all-powerful), omniscient (all-knowing) and omni-benevolent (all-good) God. That sort of god is central to orthodox Judaeo-Christian theology, where God is thought to be "that than which no greater can be conceived", in Anselm's formulation, and thus as possessing all perfections such as power, knowledge and goodness to the greatest degree possible. The early Christian writer Lactantius, in reporting the Epicurean argument, focuses on God's power and goodness (Lactant. *De Ira Dei* 13.20–22, IG I-109). According to Lactantius, the Epicureans say there are four possibilities. Either God (i) wishes to eliminate evil but cannot, or (ii) can eliminate evil but does not wish it, or (iii) neither can nor wishes to prevent evil, or (iv) both can and wishes to prevent evil. But on (i) God is weak, on (ii) God is spiteful and on (iii) God is both weak and spiteful. So the only option left that is fitting for God is (iv), but this is inconsistent with the existence of evil, since, if God both wishes to and can eliminate evil, there would be no evil.

But we should be cautious about reading this precise problem back on to the Epicureans. For one thing, as we shall see later (in Chapter 16), the Epicureans wish to assert that the gods live perfect lives but have no concern for us at all. So they would probably reject Lactantius' suggestion that gods who do not wish to eliminate evil are spiteful and thus flawed. More importantly, the Epicureans' opponents do not believe in the omni-X god of Anselmian theology. In Plato's *Timaeus*, the Craftsman is wise and extremely powerful and, being free of jealousy, he generously does his best to fashion an orderly *cosmos*. But he does not create the world *ex nihilo*; instead, he imposes form and order on a disordered mass of pre-existing stuff, and this recalcitrant matter limits how well he can do his job. Likewise, the Stoics are happy to portray god both as an animal identical to the *cosmos*, and as a craftsman who creates the *cosmos* for our benefit (e.g. Cic. *Nat D.* II 133, LS 54N). But god is still limited by the matter he uses: for example, the relative thinness and fragility of the skull is a foreseen but unintended concomitant of god's beneficent plan, as he could not make the skull any thicker without compromising our rationality (Gellius 7.1.1–13, LS 54Q).

And the main Epicurean report we have of the problem of evil, in Lucretius, does not mention omnipotence. Instead, he simply asserts that the world was not created by the gods for our benefit, because it is far too flawed (*DRN* V 195–9). He then goes on to catalogue the imperfections of the world, all of which are examples of "natural" and not "moral" evil: evils that are not the result of human choice but of the other workings of nature. For example, Lucretius notes that much of the world is inhospitable to human life, that it is difficult to raise the food we need to survive, and that drought, tornadoes or other natural disasters often destroy the crops we do raise. He then throws wild animals that devour us and terrible diseases into the unsavoury mix. Lucretius concludes his litany of troubles by remarking that newborn infants are right to cry out woefully when they first enter the world, considering the sorrows awaiting them (*DRN* V 200–227). So the Epicureans' argument has a wider target than the logical problem of evil, but they seem confident that the world is messed up enough that the argument can still succeed.

The final camp of opponents contains those who believe in the gods of the traditional Greek and Roman pantheons. The existence of these gods seems unaffected by the problem of evil, because they are not beneficent. After all, Zeus is portrayed as doing things like changing himself into a swan and raping an innocent woman. And the existence of such gods would seem far more troubling to our tranquillity than the existence of the beneficent Platonic or Stoic gods. The Epicureans have two strategies for disposing of these deities.

The first is to appeal to the idea of what it is to be a god. The Epicureans claim that our natural preconception of a god (see Ch.

10, § "Preconceptions") is of a perfectly blessed being, and perfect blessedness is inconsistent with jealousy and anger (*KD* 1). So there cannot be jealous and angry gods. This may seem to be a dubious victory by definition: even if he accepts the conclusion, the believer in the traditional pantheon could simply wave it away as a linguistic quibble and say that he still believes in the existence of Zeus, Hera and all of the others. But now he will concede that they are not "gods", but "googes": non-blessed stooges who otherwise are like gods. Still, this line of argument might have some bite, in so far as there are tensions within popular Greek religion: Zeus is portrayed both as raping women and as the lord of justice; Athena both as squabbling over a golden apple and as the exemplar of wisdom; and the like. So a traditional believer committed to the idea that the gods are admirable may be unwilling to make the reply that Zeus and Athena are merely "googes".

The second strategy is shown briefly in Lucretius' description of the thunderbolt. After giving a detailed non-teleological account of the nature of the thunderbolt (*DRN* VI 219–378), Lucretius specifically tries to debunk the idea that thunderbolts are the weapons of Jupiter (the Latin name for Zeus). Lucretius' basic point is that the distribution of thunderbolts seems not to fit into any sort of divine plan at all (good or bad), but they fall here and there for no purpose. He notes that thunderbolts fall on deserts and the sea, which would seem to be a total waste of time, although he adds sarcastically that maybe throwing them about in this way helps Jupiter get some exercise and build up his muscles. Furthermore, they hit the innocent and guilty alike (so they do not serve the purposes of Jupiter as upholder of justice), and in fact they sometimes fall on Jupiter's own shrines and statues, and those of other gods (*DRN* VI 379–422). So we have excellent reason, especially once we have a satisfying atomic and naturalistic account of the phenomenon, to reject the notion that thunderbolts occur as the result of the will of the gods.

SIX

Biology and language

As we have seen, the Epicureans try to exclude the gods from the creation and administration of the world. But to complete the job, the Epicureans need to give a non-teleological account for the formation not only of the heavenly bodies and of phenomena like thunderbolts, but also of organisms. And this is a difficult task. It is one thing to say that the thunderbolt is merely the squeezing out of seeds of fire from the collisions of clouds, and that the distribution of thunderbolts over the seas, mountains and deserts shows no pattern or purpose, quite another to say that the eye and heart exhibit no purpose. In ancient times, the apparent craftsman-like skill exhibited in the cunning organization of our bodily parts was often taken as one of the primary pieces of evidence for the existence of a wise craftsman god, and this sort of argument has persisted through William Paley and current proponents of intelligent design.

In response to this challenge, the Epicureans propose that the organisms around today are the result of a long process of natural selection, and so we can account for organisms' well-adaptedness for survival and reproduction without appealing to any sort of purpose. This explanation has been rightly compared to Charles Darwin's theory of natural selection. However, it is important not to overstate the similarity, as the Epicurean theory appeals to natural selection but without the evolution of species.

Another phenomenon sometimes attributed to the gods that the Epicureans wish to give a non-teleological explanation for is language. They offer an innovative account on which the meanings of words are not entirely a matter of contrivance. Instead, language is the product of the instincts of animals – human and non-human – to give forth various sorts of utterances in response to impressions.

Artefacts and organs

Artefacts such as knives and houses are functional items: that is, they have a job to do, such as cutting things or providing shelter. Other facts about these artefacts can largely be explained by appealing to the artefacts' functions. For instance, it is not a coincidence that some particular knife is made of steel instead of marshmallow, and that it has the shape it does (with a portion suitable for use as a handle and another with a sharp edge) rather than the shape of a chopstick; marshmallow material composition and chopstick shape would be unsuitable for cutting things. In the case of more complex artefacts such as houses, we can specify sub-parts of the house as having sub-functions of their own that allow the house as a whole to function well. Plumbing is not just a series of tubes: it has the job of transporting water around the house for the benefit of its inhabitants, which (in part) is why plumbing is made of metal or plastic rather than cardboard.

The parts of animals appear to be functional items in the same sort of way. The heart is not merely a muscle in the chest. It is a pump for blood, allowing the organism to receive nutrients and oxygen. That is why it is made of muscle (instead of bone) and is located in the chest (instead of the left foot). The hand is a grasping implement, and having an opposable thumb allows it to do its job well. Aristotle develops these sorts of functional analyses of bodily parts in the greatest detail. Because of his functional understanding of bodily organs, he would say that a hand detached from a body is not literally a hand (as it cannot do the job that makes a hand a hand), but is called a hand only homonymously; that is, it is a "hand" only in the sense that it is shaped like a hand and used to be a hand (*Part. an.* I 640b30–641a6).

The Epicurean response to this line of thought is to deny the analogy between organs and artefacts. The fact that something is *useful for the sake of X-ing* does not mean that it has the *function of X-ing* or that it was made *in order to X*. If I need to drive a tent stake into the ground and forgot to bring along my mallet, I might search around a nearby riverbed for a while until I find a suitably sized rock with a flattened side to do the job. But the flattened rock is not an artefact. It is a coincidence that it has the right size and shape for the task at hand, and its size and shape are entirely the result of non-purposive factors such as erosion by the flowing water of the stream. On the other hand, we *did* make the mallet in order to do things such as drive in tent stakes, and so features such as its material composition and shape are the result of its function (*DRN* IV 823–57, LS 13E).

If our organs had been made by skilled craftsmen gods in order to perform functions such as seeing, pumping blood and grasping things, then the analogy would go through. But as we saw in the previous chapter, the Epicureans argue that the workings of the world are not the result of any sort of divine plan. Aristotle, on the other hand, proposes an immanent teleology. He believes in gods, but does not think that organisms are the result of their plan. Nonetheless, the parts of animals exist for the sake of performing certain functions. But the Epicureans deny that this is possible: in order for something to exist for the sake of some goal, it must be the result of the intention of some agent (Simpl. *in Phys.* 198b29, IG I-111). To say that the hearts exist in order to pump blood, even though nobody made them for that purpose, makes no sense.

Natural selection

The Epicurean reply to Aristotle still leaves open the question of how we can account for the apparent design, the apparent purposiveness, of bodily organs. The Epicureans are right to insist that it does not follow from the fact that something is *useful for X-ing* that it has the *purpose of X-ing*. But in the case of the flattened rock, it seems eminently reasonably to assert that it just happens to be useful for the sake of hammering a tent stake, even though it was not made for that end. But to assert that the heart just happens to be useful for pumping blood and the hand for grasping objects appears incredible: it is just too much of a coincidence to accept.

The Epicureans respond that it is no coincidence that organisms are extremely well adapted for survival and reproduction. The animals and plants we see around today are the descendants of other animals and plants. In the past, there was a much wider variety of organisms around, but creatures with bodily set-ups less well suited for survival and reproduction died off in the competition with others. A creature with its heart located in an extremity would circulate its blood less well, and so it might be sluggish; creatures like us but without opposable thumbs could not handle tools as well as we do and so eventually starved to death; and so forth. Because of this process of natural selection, only the members of the fittest species – those that are adept at survival and reproduction within their ecological niches – are around now. Please note that this is the *result* of the process of natural selection, but not its *goal*. Natural selection is not a random process: it proceeds in a definite direction, with less fit organisms being culled over time. But it is not a purposive process either; natural selection is not trying to produce the survival of fitter species any more than a river is trying to produce smoother rocks.

The affinities of this theory with Darwin's theory are obvious, but the Epicureans are not evolutionists. Instead, all of the species we see today (plus countless others besides) were all created within a relatively short time. Lucretius is by far our fullest source for the Epicurean story. Long ago, the earth was in a fertile period and was able to act as the "mother" of animals. There was great heat and moisture, and "wombs" grew fastened to the earth, from which new creatures sprang. This probably seems less incredible to the Epicureans than to us, as they believe (along with most other Greeks and Romans) in spontaneous generation. Lucretius appeals to the (supposed) generation of new creatures in muddy warm areas even now – presumably he has worms and the like in mind – to render plausible the idea that the earth did the same sort of thing before (*DRN* V 772–825). But we do not see large and complicated creatures being hatched directly from the earth, as happened back then, because the earth used to be much more fertile, whereas now it is much colder and drier (*DRN* V 826–36).

After this initial bursting forth of new creatures comes the process of natural selection described above. According to Lucretius, many of the creatures were utterly unsuitable to live, lacking feet or hands, while others did not have reproductive organs. These all died out immediately. But later, competition among animals drove other species to extinction, with those having strength (such as lions), cunning (such as foxes) or speed (such as deer) surviving (*DRN* V 837–77).

So unlike Darwin, there is no evolution, with new species arising out of old. For Darwin, random mutations can introduce novel modifications to a creature's descendants, and there is "descent with modification", with natural selection acting on those progeny, preserving beneficial mutations and eliminating harmful ones. Enough such modifications over time can introduce huge changes, with parakeets descending from dinosaurs and human beings from tree shrews. The Epicureans do seem to accept the idea of some limited Lamarckian evolution. For Lamarck, the characteristics that a creature acquires during its lifetime can be passed on to its descendants, so that giraffes who acquire longer necks by stretching for high leaves will have longer-necked descendants, and Arnold Schwarzenegger will produce more muscular children. Lucretius says that our ancestors were stronger and tougher than we are, because being exposed to the soft living of civilization has caused us to become weaker and less able to withstand extreme conditions (*DRN* V 925–1027). But there is no suggestion that these changes would be sufficient to make a new species arise.

The spontaneous generation from the earth of many complex organisms, such as elephants, may seem highly unlikely. The process of abiogenesis (how living things arise from non-living things) is still not understood fully today, but it seems less incredible if the first organisms are fairly simple. The Epicureans could reply that this spontaneous generation need not be likely, it need only be *possible*. Given the infinity of time and space, if it is possible, it will occur. And once it occurs, it is not at all a coincidence that we happen to live on such a world, one of the tiny fraction of worlds suited to produce complex life like us.

Still, there are limits on what is physically possible. The Epicurean theory is heavily indebted to a similar theory advanced by the Presocratic philosopher Empedocles, who also asserts that during a fertile period of the world a great variety of misshapen creatures was produced, with this variety subsequently being whittled down. But for Empedocles, some of these primitive creatures were random bodily parts from different types of organisms stuck together, and even individual organs (detached heads and the like).[1] Lucretius goes out of his way to argue that such creatures, as well as chimeras, centaurs and the other mixed creatures of mythology, cannot occur. Even spontaneously generated organisms do not come together all at once. Instead, they are the result of a process of biological development, the unfolding of "seeds" within the womb. So they must meet some minimal threshold of "hanging together" properly to come into existence, even if they are not suitable for surviving or reproducing well. A centaur is a combination of two incompatible types of creatures – man and horse – with different rates of maturation, different nutritional requirements and differing metabolisms. Poorly put-together creatures – people with no limbs, or dogs with no genitalia – are physically possible, but hodge-podge creatures are not, any more than are trees bearing jewels as fruit or rivers running with gold (*DRN* V 877–924).

Language

One phenomenon that the Epicureans need to account for is language. The Epicureans regard language as above all else a biological phenomenon, and they stress the continuities between human language and the sounds instinctively made by other animals. Thus, discussing the Epicurean theory of language at the end of a chapter dealing with their biology makes some sense, whereas for most philosophers this placement would be extremely odd. One welcome consequence of being able to give a biological account of the origins and nature of language is that it allows us to dismiss the superstitious belief that language is a gift of the gods, such as Hermes (Diogenes of Oinoanda 10.2.11 ff., LS 19C).

However, it appears that there is another way of accounting for language that allows us not to attribute it to the gods, that is, to regard it as a human invention. According to this sort of theory, the names of things are assigned by convention. So, for instance, I want to have a way to refer to "that sort of thing over there", and I coin the word "dog" to do the job. If our group adopts the name, then the word "dog" means dog for us because of this convention. (Aristotle champions the conventionalist position; see *Int.* 2.) This sort of theory does not invoke the gods. And as we shall see (Chapter 14), the Epicureans regard justice as a kind of artefact that comes into existence as a result of our adopting a convention about how to behave. So there would seem to be little reason in principle for them not to adopt an analogous position with regard to language.

Nonetheless, they object to the conventionalist account. Lucretius writes that it would be impossible for us to learn our first words by some person conventionally assigning a name to something. After all, unless the "original namer" had already acquired from somewhere the idea that you can use sounds to name things, he never would have started the practice. And leaving that problem aside, if his audience members did not already have the idea that sounds can express things, his efforts to establish a convention would be utterly unsuccessful; it would be like talking to a deaf crowd, as they would simply be confused and annoyed by his blurting out the senseless sound "dog!" and pointing (*DRN* V 1041–55).

Instead, meaningful human language has its origins in animal utterances. Dogs emit one kind of yelp when in pain, another when angry, another when playfully nipping their puppies. Different sorts of impressions – both impressions of external objects (such as a potential sexual partner or a predator) and of internal ones (such as a stinging pain) – naturally evoke different sorts of utterances. This sort of natural language can be found among dogs, birds and horses, and so it is plausible to suppose that the same sort of thing occurred among primitive human beings too (*DRN* V 1056–90).

A certain sort of dog yelp "means" pain because it is characteristically *caused by* the dog's being in pain. And likewise with the meaning of the other animal utterances ("Lo! A predator", "Lo! An object of sexual interest", etc.). So the Epicureans assimilate linguistic meaning to what Paul Grice much later dubs "natural meaning": the sense in which "smoke means fire" or "spots mean measles". In the same sort of way, "that kind of yelp means the dog is in pain". Grice himself sharply distinguishes linguistic meaning from natural meaning, thinking that statements have a "non-natural meaning" that should be analysed in terms of a speaker's intentions to communicate with an audience (Grice 1957). The Epicureans, of course, do not want to deny that language can be used intentionally to communicate with an audience, but they would be loathe to sharply distinguish the two types of meaning. Instead, our ability to use language to communicate intentionally has its roots in the natural meaning of instinctive animal sounds.

Likewise, they would not want to sharply distinguish (as do the Stoics) between human language and animal bellows. For the Stoics, our statements express propositions (*lekta*).[2] So when a human being says "I am in pain", he understands the meaning of the phrase and uses the sentence to express this proposition to somebody. On the other hand, when a dog sharply yelps after being beaten by Descartes with a stick, he *expresses* his pain but does not state *that* he is in pain (*DL* 7.55–6, LS 33H). The Epicureans would admit that there is typically a level of complexity and self-awareness in human speech lacking in dog yelps but deny any radical discontinuity in the sense in which the two are meaningful.

Although the origins of human language and its meaning can be found in natural utterances that are responses to stimuli, the Epicureans allow that convention plays a large role. Once we have names for things established naturally, then people can extend and refine language. They can agree to new coinages to express things less ambiguously and more concisely, or to name things that previously had no name. In response to the objection that the conventionalist theory is better able to account for the diversity of languages (e.g. even simple natural impressions such as "pain" are designated by wildly different sounds), Epicurus responds that the uncontrived "natural" utterances of primitive peoples could have varied from tribe to tribe depending on their environments and physique (*Ep. Hdt.* 75–6).

SEVEN

The mind

The mind, a bodily organ

The Epicureans assert that the mind is a part of the body, no less than a hand or an eye (*DRN* III 94ff.). Just as the heart is the bodily organ responsible for pumping blood through the body, so too the mind is the bodily organ responsible for sensation, thought and memory (*Ep. Hdt.* 63).

The Epicurean theory obviously has affinities to current identity theories of mind, but the physiology is different. Whereas current identity theorists identify the mind with the brain, Epicurus goes along with the view, common (although not universally held) at his time, of locating it in the chest. Lucretius argues for this location by noting that the centre of the chest is where we feel fear, dread and joy; think of the gaping feeling there when you are startled, for instance (*DRN* III 136–44).[1] Likewise, just as mental processes are identified with neural processes by current identity theorists, the Epicureans identify mental processes with atomic processes, for example the raving that accompanies epilepsy occurs because the atoms that constitute the mind are being tossed about like water frothing during a storm (*DRN* III 487–95). The mind is made up of four different sorts of particles: heat, air, wind and a nameless fourth element (Aëtius 4.3.11, LS 14C, *DRN* III 231–57). Although they are reticent about the details, the Epicureans do try to explain some mental properties in terms of the properties of these individual elements; for example, heat particles are responsible for the heat of anger, and calm air for tranquillity. The nameless "fourth element" accounts for sensation, and Lucretius says it must be especially small and smooth, to account for the quickness of thought and the ability of the mind to be easily moved by images, which themselves are fine atomic films emitted from the surfaces of objects (*DRN* III 238–45).

In addition to the mind proper, there is a mind-like "spirit" (*anima* in Latin) spread throughout the body, that allows the mind to communicate with the rest of the body: to receive information from the body and to send out impulses to it. If the mind for the Epicureans is like the brain, then the "spirit" is like the secondary nervous system.

A brief terminological digression: I have been speaking, and shall continue to speak, about the Epicurean views on the mind, usually using "mind" to translate the Greek *psyche* and Latin *animus.* I avoid the more common translation of "soul" for *psyche*, as the English word "soul" currently has connotations that do not apply to the Epicurean views of what the *psyche* is. For some other authors, such as Plato, the translation of *psyche* as soul is more natural, as Plato argues that the *psyche* is something immortal and immaterial, which flits from body to body in a cycle of reincarnation, with your conduct in this life determining how well you will do in the next. Aristotle uses the term quite broadly to encompass the organizing principle that distinguishes living from non-living things, so that, for Aristotle, a plant has a *psyche* without having a mind. For Epicurus, the *psyche* is the thing that is responsible for functions such as perceiving, thinking and making choices. Saying that the Epicureans believe that the mind is a bodily organ straightforwardly expresses their basic view, whereas saying that they believe that the *soul* is a bodily organ sounds bizarre, and would unnecessarily muddy the waters.

The main Epicurean argument for believing that the mind is something bodily is based on the causal interaction of the mind and body, as follows (*DRN* III 163–87):

1. The mind moves the body and is moved by the body.
2. Only bodies can move and be moved by other bodies.

---

3. Therefore, the mind is a body.

Actions show that the mind moves the body. I decide to walk to the refrigerator to grab a bite to eat, and lo! my body moves. Another way in which the mind moves the body would be the physiological effects of emotional states, for example the flushing and tightness I sometimes get in my neck when I become upset. Sensations show that the body moves the mind. A swift kick in the shin moves my body, and in turn my body moves my mind as I feel pain: the bodily changes cause a change in my mind.

The second premise is a bit more contentious. Lucretius says that only bodies can act or be acted on by other bodies because all action and reaction must occur *by contact*, and that only bodies can touch and be touched (*DRN* III 161–7). That is, one body can move another by banging into it and pushing it along, and only bodies – which are tangible – can do this sort of thing. Epicurus says that the mind cannot be incorporeal. That is because the only thing that is incorporeal is the void. But the void cannot do or suffer anything; it just allows bodies to pass through it (*Ep. Hdt.* 67).

In addition to the general phenomenon of the mind and body interacting, the particular ways in which the mind depends on the body helps reinforce the thesis that the mind is something bodily. Lucretius notes that the mind grows with the body, declines with the body, and is subject to diseases just as the body is (*DRN* III 445–525).[2] A person's mind is undeveloped at birth, along with the rest of his body, and slowly grows and matures. The damage caused by a stroke can destroy a person's memories and change his personality, and we now know that the protein deposits along the neurons that occur because of Alzheimer's disease do so too. Alcohol ingestion often makes people feel more witty and clever while making them actually less witty and clever. All of these things are exactly what we would expect if the mind is a bodily organ, whereas if the mind were some separable and incorporeal entity that (somehow) was in communication with the body, none of this should occur.

Death, the permanent end of one's existence

The Epicureans are keen to establish that the mind is a bodily organ not merely because they wish to fit an important natural phenomenon within their materialistic world-view. Additionally, this thesis is the basis for their arguments that death is annihilation, which in turn is central in their therapeutic arguments that death is not bad and should not be feared. Since the body obviously disintegrates in death, Greeks who believe in an afterlife typically think that the mind/soul – the *psyche* – survives the death of the body. Homer depicts the majority of the dead as milling about in a gloomy, shadowy half-existence, with some evil-doers singled out for elaborate eternal punishments and a few heroes of divine descent enjoying bliss in Elysium, while Plato and the Pythagoreans describe the *psyche* as being reincarnated in another creature. Accordingly, the Epicurean arguments try to establish that on death the *psyche* ceases functioning along with the rest of the body.

It is easy to see why death would be annihilation if the mind is identical to the brain. The brain is a bodily organ that needs to be housed in a living body to survive. On death, it dies along with the rest of the body. The matter that makes up the brain continues to exist, but it is no longer matter making up a functioning brain, but a slowly putrefying hunk composed of atoms. And without a mind, there can be no thinking, memory, consciousness or character traits. The person who used to exist is forever no more; death is annihilation.

Once we take differences of physiology into account, the basic Epicurean argument is fairly similar. The mind is a group of fine atoms trapped in the chest. On death, the "container" of the body cannot hold those atoms in as it did before, and the mind disintegrates, as the atoms making it up escape into the surrounding air (*DRN* III 425–44). An eye or a nose detached from the body cannot sense anything, or even really exist as an eye or a nose. Instead, they quickly decompose. Likewise, the mind can engage in "sensory motions" only when it is confined in the proper way in a living body. Death is the permanent dissolution of body and mind (*DRN* III 548–79).

This argument is quite powerful, but the thesis that death is annihilation is important enough to secure that Lucretius piles up a host of subsidiary arguments for it. He is also happy to try to discredit the Platonic idea that souls pre-exist their bodies and enter them on conception by mocking it. He says it is ridiculous to imagine a bunch of immortal souls fighting each other at the couplings of wild beasts, trying to be the first to get in; Lucretius facetiously suggests that maybe they would agree to a "first come, first served" policy to avoid the struggle (*DRN* III 776–83). We shall not go through all of the subsidiary arguments here, but two that turn on issues of personal identity are worth considering further.

The first argument is concessive: *even if* the mind survives the death of the body, *we* do not survive, because we are a union of mind and body (*DRN* III 843–6). Consider the argument for immortality near the end of Plato's *Phaedo*, for instance (*Phd.* 102b–107a): for it to succeed, Socrates should establish not only that the *psyche* is essentially alive and so can never die, but also that I am my *psyche*. But Lucretius denies this: I am a human being, a living animal that is a union of mind and body. So even if *it* goes on and survives my death, *I* do not survive my death.

While this brief argument seems to rely on a biological criterion of bodily continuity as necessary for personal identity, elsewhere Lucretius appeals to psychological considerations to undercut the Platonic position. For instance, Lucretius argues that the mind does not pre-exist the body because if it did, it should have memories of its past existence, which it does not. He then adds, though, that if the mind did lose all memories on birth, such a total transformation of the mind is not all that different from death anyway (*DRN* III 670–78). Although he does not explicitly do so, Lucretius could have used this sort of argument against the Platonic theory that the *psyche* goes on to another life. For the sake of argument, let us grant that my *psyche* transmigrates after my death and animates the body of a poor factory-farmed chicken, in retribution for my own callous consumption of chicken nuggets. Since there will be no links of memory or personality between me and the chicken, there is little reason for me to think that the chicken's suffering will be bad for *me*, any more than the suffering of some unknown peasant in the Middle Ages that my *psyche* inhabited was bad for me.

Lucretius appeals to considerations of both biological and psychological continuity when considering the possibility that all of the atoms that constitute me could eventually reassemble and recreate me (*DRN* III 847–61). Given the infinity of time and space, the Epicureans should grant that this may happen, and it seems to give a plausible ground for post-mortem survival without requiring the soul to survive the death of the body. Lucretius grants the possibility of this re-creation happening, but he denies that this person would be *me*, rather than an exact duplicate of me. There is a gap of life between me and that future person, a time during which the atoms wandered about not engaging in the motions of sensation, so that when they come back together they form a new creature. Furthermore, there will be no links of memory or consciousness between me and that future person, so that his life is nothing more to me than are the past lives of those past selves I cannot remember at all.

Reason and the reality of the mental[3]

As we shall see (Chapter 11), Epicurean psychology is hedonistic, with pleasure and pain motivating all of our actions. Given that you desire pleasure, and you believe that doing *X* will bring you pleasure more effectively than any other available course of action, you will do *X*. This psychological hedonism does not threaten our freedom, however, because our beliefs are under our control. We can modify such desires that would lead to unhappiness by using our reason. We can discover the limits of pleasure and distinguish natural and necessary desires, merely natural desires, and vain and empty desires (*KD* 18–22, 29–30). We can ask, of every desire we have, "what will happen if I get what I desire, and what will happen if I do not?" (*SV* 71). Using our reason, we can overcome hate, envy and contempt (*DL* X 117). Reason allows us to do this by showing us that certain desires, temperaments and ways of life are not effective for getting us what we ultimately desire for its own sake, that is, pleasure.

This reasons-responsiveness distinguishes us from other animals. Human beings can control their own development, while non-human animals cannot. Lucretius gives the clearest Epicurean statement of this doctrine. For example, lions are naturally irascible because their souls contain many fire atoms; stags are timid because they have more wind atoms (*DRN* III 288ff.). People also have natural temperaments: some are naturally easily moved to anger, while others are too fearful (*DRN* III 307–19). These differences cannot be erased entirely, but the traces of these natural temperaments that remain beyond the power of reason to expel are so trivial that they do nothing to impede our living a life worthy of the gods (*DRN* III 320–22).

Other Epicureans such as Hermarchus and Polystratus also assert that it is our reasoning abilities that set us apart from other animals. We can calculate the outcomes of different possible courses of action, whereas animals have only "irrational memory", that is, they have repeated experiences that can condition them to act in certain ways, and to find certain things attractive or repulsive, but they do not explicitly think through the outcomes of what they may do. That is because they do not have prudential concepts such as "healthy" and "expedient", and they cannot make causal inferences.[4]

So Epicurus needs to account for the emergence and causal efficacy of things such as human reason, plus other psychological phenomena, within an atomistic worldview. Epicurus' efforts here are spurred by the troubles he thinks were encountered by Democritus.

We have already looked (in Chapter 4) at the ways in which Epicurus modified Democritus' ontology in order to escape sceptical difficulties. Because properties like sweetness are not intrinsic properties of bodies, and because they are mutable and do not exist at the level of the individual atom, Democritus eliminates them from his ontology. He declares that they exist only "by convention", and that honey is no more sweet than it is bitter because in reality it is neither. Epicurus responds that this does not follow: atomic aggregates have properties and powers that individual atoms do not. In order to account for these properties and powers, we often need to look to the structural features of aggregates, which arise because of the spatial relations holding between the atoms that constitute the aggregate, the ways in which they have become entangled with one another, and so forth. These properties and powers are real, and include relational properties such as being enslaved, being healthy or being sweet.

Now on to the mind. Epicureans think (perhaps wrongly) that Democritus' eliminativism extends far beyond sensible qualities. Plutarch's *Against Colotes* gives the fullest statement of this Epicurean charge against Democritus. In his version of Democritus' famous saying "By convention, <this, that, and the other,> in reality atoms and void" (DK 68 B9), the Epicurean Colotes includes *compounds* among the things that are for Democritus merely "by convention" and says that anybody who believes this could not conceive of himself as a human or as alive, presumably because human beings are compound bodies (*Adv. Col.* 1110e).

On this understanding of Democritus' ontology, Democritus remains close to the Eleatics like Parmenides. For the Eleatics, the realm of Being is the realm of what is ungenerated, imperishable and changeless. As we have seen, Democritean and Epicurean atoms basically meet these Parmenidean requirements for Being, changing only in their locations, motions and relationships to other atoms. The mutable and temporary objects of sensation, however, do not conform to these requirements, and for both Parmenides and Democritus they are relegated to the deceptive and ultimately illusory realm of Becoming.

Plutarch agrees with this radical interpretation of Democritus' ontology, and he spells out the eliminative position as follows: atoms flying through the void collide and entangle with one another, and the resulting atomic aggregates may *appear* to be water, or fire, or a human, but in reality nothing other than atoms and the void exists. Plutarch notes that a result of this is that colours and the mind do not exist. So Epicurus also needs to find a way of defending the reality of the mind and of mental properties against the threat of Democritean eliminativism.[5]

But the same sort of reply is available to the Epicureans in the case of compound bodies generally, and the mind in particular, as it is in the case of sensible qualities: once we understand the meaning of predicates such as *being heating* it would be naive to think that properties such as being heating are unreal just because they are relative. Likewise, in the case of macroscopic bodies, Epicurus himself regularly refers to them as being merely aggregates of atoms, but he refuses to draw the conclusion that, as atomic aggregates, they are somehow unreal.[6] Epicurus admits that some things (atoms and void) are indestructible and unchanging, while others (aggregates and their properties) are generated and mutable, but Colotes insists that Epicurus is wiser than Plato in applying the name "beings" (*onta*) equally to all of them alike (*Adv. Col.* 1116c–d).

To put it in resolutely anachronistic terms, let us imagine a group of atoms arranged tablewise: Democritus (on the Epicurean interpretation) will say "we thought that there was a genuine object there, a table, but this is mistaken; in reality there is just a bunch of atoms arranged tablewise, nothing else".[7] The Epicureans, on the other hand, will say that a macroscopic object such as a table can be *identified* with a bunch of atoms arranged tablewise and, as such, is perfectly real. Likewise with the mind.

This response to Democritus need commit Epicurus to an "emergent" view of the mind in a weak sense only. That is, the mind is real, and it is "emergent" in the sense that has powers and properties that none of its constituent atoms do. This sense of emergence, however, is consistent with identifying the mind with a bodily organ that is nothing more than an atomic aggregate, and with identifying mental events with bodily events that are explained in terms of the motions of the atoms that compose the mind.

And the Epicureans appear to advance such a view, as the texts we have discussed above (§ "The mind, a bodily organ") point towards an identity theory of the mind. However, this interpretation is contentious: it is clear that Epicurus wishes to preserve the reality of the mental (and of our reason, in particular) against the threat of Democritean eliminative materialism, but it is less widely accepted that he counters this threat by reaffirming the mind's reality within an identity theory. The controversies largely centre on how to understand the extant portions of book twenty-five of *On Nature*, Epicurus' *magnum opus*. The passages we have contain a description of human psychological development, including the relationship between psychological states and the atoms that constitute the mind.

Going into detail on these issues would far exceed the scope of this chapter.[8] The text is in terrible shape (it was buried in the eruption of Mount Vesuvius in 79 CE) and bristles with unexplained technical terminology. It is hard to overstate its obscurity. In it, Epicurus asserts that psychological "products" arise, and it is these products, and *not* the nature of the atoms, that are responsible for a person developing in the particular way he does. These products differ from the atoms in a "differential" way, and they acquire the "cause out of itself", which then reaches as far as the "first natures".[9] My best guess as to what any of this means, so that it is consistent with the other texts we have, is that we can *distinguish* the psychological products and the atoms of the mind in thought, even though the product is just an aspect of the atomic aggregate. However, once we do so, we see that the proper way to explain why people acquire the characters they do, for example why somebody is irascible, is by referring to the operations of these complicated psychological developments, not to the natures of the atoms that constitute the mind. For instance, an explanation of why some adult grew up to become a hothead will be a complicated story referring to his beliefs, environment, ideals and so on, not just to the preponderance of fiery atoms in his mind. Our ability to shape our own character reaches as far as our "first natures", that is to the congenital dispositions Lucretius discusses as amenable to reason.

However, on the basis of these passages, others have seen Epicurus as abandoning an identity theory of mind in order to preserve the reality and causal efficacy of the mental. On this view, the operations of reason and other psychological states cannot be identified with atomic processes, even though they arise only when atoms are suitably arranged to constitute a mind. These emergent psychological states then gain causal *independence* (the "cause out of itself") from the atoms that constitute the mind; what they do is not determined by the atoms that make up the mind. Furthermore, they exert "downwards causation" and move the soul's atoms (the "first natures"), that is, they are able to reach "down" from the psychological to the atomic level and change the arrangement of the atoms of the mind.[10] I think that this interpretation is too starkly inconsistent with Epicurus' overall materialistic metaphysics, as well as the Epicurean writings on the mind in particular, to be correct. However, if Epicurus did think he had to choose between materialism and the reality and causal efficacy of the mental, he would kiss materialism goodbye. It is evident that the mind exists and moves the body, and any theory must comport with what is evident.

EIGHT

Freedom and determinism

The Epicureans wish to preserve human freedom in a world whose ultimate constituents are just extended bits of stuff flying around in empty space. And in order to do so, they famously posit an indeterministic atomic motion: the swerve. While their use of the swerve to preserve our freedom is intriguing, it was subject to withering criticisms by their Academic and Stoic opponents.

Lucretius and "free will"

How our freedom is threatened by determinism, and how the swerve is supposed to counter this threat, are unfortunately obscure; nothing even close to a consensus view of what the Epicurean position is supposed to be has emerged.[1] In part that is because the swerve is not even mentioned in the extant writings of Epicurus, so we have to rely on later reports in order to try to piece together Epicurus' position. Lucretius presents the most extended consideration we have by an Epicurean of the swerve and freedom (*DRN* II 251–93). It comes immediately after his argument that the swerve must exist in order for atoms to collide. Atoms naturally fall straight downwards, and they also move because of collisions and entanglements with other atoms. However, there is a third cause of atomic motion, a random swerve to the side by one spatial minimum, which saves us from what Lucretius calls the "decrees of fate". His basic argument goes as follows:

1. If atoms did not swerve, there would not be "free volition" (*libera voluntas*).
2. There is free volition.

---

3. Therefore, atoms swerve.

The argument follows the same familiar Epicurean pattern as the argument for void and the first argument for the swerve's existence. Each argument starts from something evident in perception, such as the existence of motion or of compound bodies, and on its basis infers a conclusion about what is not directly accessible to perception, such as void or the swerve. In this passage, Lucretius says that we cannot directly perceive individual atomic swerves, but that animals act freely, which we can see, allows us to infer that they exist.

Lucretius writes that an occasional random atomic swerve initiates new motion, which prevents the existence of an endless chain of atomic causation, of new motion unalterably arising out of old. This swerve annuls the decrees of fate and allows us to have free volition.

But how is that supposed to work? Lucretius does not tell us, but a natural line of interpretation is the following:[2] Epicurus appropriates most of his metaphysics and physics from Democritus, including the identification of the mind with a bodily organ, an atomic aggregate. However, he recognizes that Democritus' atomism has unacceptable deterministic consequences. If all atomic motions are causally necessitated, then our decisions, which are identical to atomic motions in our minds, would likewise be causally necessary, as would the actions that flow from those decisions.

On this interpretation, what is wrong with this possibility is that we must have the ability to do otherwise than we do in order to be free and morally responsible. For example, imagine that a student insults my fashion sense, and I angrily punch him in the face. If Democritus were right, then given the disposition of my mind at the time, plus the (atomic) stimulus of hearing the student insulting me, my punching him in the face would be causally necessary. But then, I would not be able to do anything other than punch him in the face and, if that were so, I did not act freely, and I am not morally responsible for punching him.

To avoid this problem, Epicurus introduces the swerve, an indeterministic atomic motion, which allows him to deny that all atomic motions are causally determined. The decisions that produce our actions are identical to swerves that occur in our minds. After I hear the student insult me, an atomic swerve – or maybe a series of atomic swerves – occurs in my mind and initiates my action of punching him in the face. Thus, I did not have to punch him in the face; if the decision/swerve producing that action had not occurred, or had occurred at a different time, I would have acted differently, and so I acted freely and can be held responsible for what I do.

If this interpretation is right, Epicurus would be rightly hailed (or derided) as one of the first people to formulate the problem of free will and determinism, and to offer a libertarian response to it.[3] The problem of free will and determinism concerns the charge that causal determinism threatens our ability to do otherwise than we do, and that we must have this ability in order to be morally responsible for our actions. A libertarian believes that causal determinism and the ability to do other are incompatible with one another, while affirming that we do have free will, and so he rejects causal determinism.

Some of Lucretius' language suggests this interpretation. He declares that *libera voluntas* is incompatible with determinism. While I have been rendering this phrase by "free volition", a more common translation is "free will". Furthermore, Lucretius draws an analogy between our free will and the atomic swerve; just as the atoms have the ability to initiate new motion by swerving, so too we can swerve off our course at no fixed time or place, wherever we wish. This analogy is easy to understand if our decisions are atomic swerves: we "swerve" like the atoms do because our decisions are atomic swerves.

Despite these attractions, the preceding line of interpretation suffers from some serious problems, both philosophical and textual.

The philosophical problem is that a random atomic swerving in one's mind is an unpromising basis for the production of free and responsible actions, instead of random and blameless twitches.[4] Let us imagine that I am an Epicurean sage, and when the student insults my beloved but ratty T-shirts, I realize that a concern for fashion would be a vain and empty desire, and catering to the opinions of the many on this topic leads to unnecessary disturbance. As I prepare to walk away calmly, however, a random atomic swerve occurs, and I punch him in the face instead. Having random, uncaused swerves intervene between my desires and beliefs and the actions prompted by them would undercut rather than preserve my control over what I do. And within Epicureanism, it is difficult to see why being able to randomly swerve off in my actions occasionally in this way would be regarded as a valuable ability to be preserved rather than a crippling disability to be guarded against. There may be cases in which the results of the swerve happen to align with my beliefs and desires, but this would just be a lucky coincidence, it seems. It is hard to construct any story about the role of the swerve in which it actually helps makes actions more under the control of the agent, instead of merely sometimes not undercutting that control too much.

The textual problems are twofold. Less serious is an argument from silence: if swerves played a central role in the production of free actions, we would expect Lucretius to mention them in his account of how volition arises and moves the body, but he does not.[5]

More seriously, the "free volition" that Lucretius describes as preserved by the swerve bears little resemblance to the "ability to do otherwise than one does" that figures prominently in the problem of free will and determinism described above.

Lucretius spends most of his argument (*DRN* II 261–83) illustrating why its second premise ("there is free volition") is supposed to be obviously true, and in so doing, he shows what sort of "free volition" determinism threatens. Free volition is what allows creatures throughout the earth, both human and non-human, to do what they want to do and to advance wherever pleasure leads them. Lucretius establishes that free volition exists by showing that the body follows the mind's desire. He gives two examples. Both are meant to show that animals have an internal capacity to initiate or resist motion, and that this capacity distinguishes animal motion from the way in which inanimate objects are shoved around by external blows. Voluntary motion has an "internal source" in the literal sense of being produced by the animal's mind, an organ in its chest.

The first example is of racehorses eager to burst from the gates (*DRN* II 263–71). Lucretius claims that we see a slight delay between the external stimulus of the gates' opening and the resultant motion of the horses surging forward. This delay supposedly shows that motion initiated by the mind exists, as it takes some time for the mind's decision to move all of the matter of the horse in a coordinated manner. Motion caused by external blows, on the other hand, does not require time for internal processing: a horse struck from behind by another horse is immediately pushed forwards.

The second example (*DRN* II 272–83) appeals to our own experience of situations such as being in a jostling crowd: we are not always helplessly shoved around by these outside forces but can sometimes fight against them to go where we wish. Imagine being carried down a river by its swift current unwillingly, sharp rocks looming downstream. Unlike an inanimate object, such as a log, we need not allow ourselves to be carried along but can fight against the current and swim for the shore in order to avoid danger.

The sort of freedom at stake here may be dubbed "effective agency". Two differences between it and "free will" (as the phrase is often used) are worth underlining. First, effective agency is possessed by all animals that can do what they wish, including many that do not have the rational capacities needed to be rightly praised or blamed; many animals possess effective agency that do not have "free will". Secondly, "effective agency" need *not* involve the ability to do otherwise than one does. The horses Lucretius describes at the starting gates are not trying to decide *whether or not* to break from the gates, and a man caught in a current is not concerned with *whether or not* to swim for the shore. Instead, as Lucretius portrays it, free volition is what allows them to move around in the world in order to obtain what they desire.

So even though Lucretius may seem initially to be saying that the swerve is needed to allow us to be able to do otherwise than we do, with our decisions being identified with atomic swerves, there are good reasons to doubt this. Instead, swerves are somehow needed for all animals to pursue pleasure.

"Effective agency" and the principle of bivalence

As Lucretius portrays it, then, *libera voluntas* is what allows us to be effective agents, to act as we wish to in order to get what we desire. However, he does little to explain how causal determinism threatens its existence, or how introducing a random atomic swerve overcomes this threat. For that, we need to turn to Cicero's *On Fate*, which describes a debate between the Epicureans, Stoics and Academic Sceptics on issues of fate and freedom.

One of its central topics is the "lazy argument", one member of a family of arguments, including the argument concerning tomorrow's sea battle in Aristotle's *De Interpretatione* 9, that try to show that accepting the universal applicability of the principle of bivalence would have unacceptable consequences on our agency. The principle of bivalence is the thesis that every proposition either is true or is false, including propositions about what will occur in the future. The type of determinism at issue here we might dub "logical" determinism".[6] Here is a sketch of how the "lazy argument" from bivalence goes. You are sick, and you are trying to decide whether or not to call a doctor. However, if you accept the principle of bivalence, then either it is true, and has always been true, that you are going to recover from the disease, or false (and always false) that you will recover, and hence always true that you will not recover (*Fat.* 29). But if either of two alternatives has been true from all eternity, that alternative is also necessary (*Fat.* 21), because the past is immutable (*Fat.* 19–20, 21, 28, 29). And because there is no point in deliberating about what is necessary, then it is pointless for me to worry now about whether or not to call the doctor, as if my present actions could change the outcome one way or the other (*Fat.* 28–9).

So, logical determinism is apparently incompatible with the contingency of the future, where this contingency is necessary for the effectiveness of deliberation and action. Epicurus asserts that it is obvious we engage in effective action and deliberation, that the future is therefore contingent, and accordingly he rejects "logical" determinism (i.e. he rejects the principle of bivalence). The "lazy argument" is quite different from the problem of free will and determinism described above, but if we keep the differences between the two in mind, we would not go too wrong in describing Epicurus as a "lazy argument libertarian".

Causal considerations are not present in the lazy argument as I have described it. However, in order to escape the "necessity of fate" that this argument would establish, Epicurus posits the atomic swerve (*Fat.* 22; see also 18, 48). He does so because he thinks that logical and causal determinism are inter-entailing; let us call this the "inter-entailment thesis". Both Epicurus and the Stoics say that things that will be true must have causes of their future being (*Fat.* 26; see also 19). The point is that, since the future is not yet – it has not obtained – there is not yet anything there in virtue of which a statement about the future can be true, unless there presently obtain conditions to bring about the state of affairs described by the statement. (Likewise, for a statement about the future to be false now, there must presently obtain conditions to preclude the state of affairs described by the statement.)

Consider a statement such as "Tim will die from his disease". My death cannot make it true, as it has not yet occurred. For the statement to be true right now, there must obtain conditions *at present* sufficient to bring it about; for example, my skin cancer has metastasized throughout my body and made my death from the disease inevitable. If you are a "lazy argument libertarian" like Epicurus and accept the inter-entailment thesis, you need some sort of physical mechanism – like the swerve – to underwrite the rejection of the principle of bivalence. The swerve allows him to admit that statements such as "Tim will die" are already true (because, as a human being, there at present obtain conditions sufficient to ensure that I will die) whereas many statements like "Tim will die of such-and-such a disease" are for now neither true nor false, as their truth is not yet settled.

If it were already true either that "Tim will die from his disease" or "Tim will not die from the disease", then it would be pointless to deliberate over which of the two to make true. But the swerve allows me to escape the necessity of fate. What will occur is not yet settled, and because the future is open in this way, I am free to decide to do as I wish in my pursuit of pleasure.

Academic criticisms of Epicurus

Carneades (214–129 BCE), the most prominent head of the sceptical Academy, makes two astute criticisms of the Epicurean position described above. The first is to deny the inter-entailment thesis. Carneades unequivocally accepts the principle of bivalence for all propositions, at all times: statements such as "Jimi Hendrix dies of a drug overdose" are eternally true (*Fat.* 37). He denies, however, that any deterministic consequences follow from the principle of bivalence, because the truth of a statement does not imply that there are "immutable eternal causes" that *make* it true (*Fat.* 28). Instead, if somebody were to say in 1965, "Jimi Hendrix will die of an overdose", it is simply the fact that Jimi Hendrix will actually die of an overdose that makes the statement true. And now we know that a person who said that in 1965 did say something true, because things turned out as the person said they would.[7]

This, however, would not satisfy the Stoics and Epicurus, who would ask in virtue of what it *was* a fact that Hendrix would die, if there were not any causes obtaining at that time to make it a fact that this would occur. In order to defend his position, Carneades appeals to the symmetry of the past and future: just as something being true in the past does not depend on its having certain effects now, something being true in the future does not depend on its having certain causes now (*Fat.* 27). If somebody were to say in 2010, "Jimi Hendrix did die of an overdose", it is simply the fact that Jimi Hendrix did actually die of an overdose that makes the statement true.

We can imagine, especially in an indeterministic world, certain past events whose effects are "washed out" over time: for example some atom decayed far in the past, at time *t*, and the present state of the world is compatible with that atom decaying either at that moment or at time $t + 0.001$s. We would then say not that there used to be a determinate truth about what time the atom decayed, but that since then it has become indeterminate whether the atom decayed at time *t* or not.

Therefore, Carneades thinks, logical determinism does not imply causal determinism. Carneades rejects the lazy argument, when it is stated in terms of truth, because the fact that it has always been *true* that something will occur does not make its occurrence necessary or inevitable in any way. If Carneades is right, then what I do now *can* have an effect on the past, in an attenuated sense. If the necessity of the past is tied to its irrevocability, then there *is* an asymmetry between the past and the future, in so far as I can affect the future, and not the past. I can kill myself today or tomorrow; I cannot kill myself yesterday. However, by my present actions, I can make it *to have been true* that something was going to occur. If I commit suicide, I make the statement "Tim O'Keefe is going to kill himself" to *have been true* in the past. If it is simply my freely deciding to blow my brains out that makes it to have always been the case that I would kill myself at that time, and thus for the statement "Tim O'Keefe will kill himself" to have been true for an eternity before I pulled the trigger, the eternal truth of that statement does nothing to threaten my freedom.

This brings us to Carneades' second criticism. Like Epicurus, Carneades rejects causal determinism, because he thinks it is incompatible with there being a voluntary movement of the mind and with anything being in our power (*Fat.* 19, 28, 38). Carneades denies that even Apollo can foreknow events such as Oedipus killing his father (although it has always been *true* that he would do so). That is because such actions, before they occurred, had no pre-existing causes that would inevitably bring them about, such that Apollo could inspect the conditions at the time in order to tell that the actions are going to occur (*Fat.* 32–3).

Carneades agrees with Epicurus that if there were pre-existing causes determining what will occur, then no actions would be in our power, and we would be helpless. So when restated in terms of causal determinism instead of logical determinism, the lazy argument is powerful (*Fat.* 31). But he then rightly says that positing a motion without a cause, like the swerve, would be beside the point in solving the problem. Carneades' solution is to say that all events, including human actions, have causes. However, voluntary actions do not have antecedent causes stretching back eternally to past events and states of affairs. Instead, these actions are simply the result of a "voluntary motion of the mind", a motion that has an intrinsic nature of being in our power and of obeying us (*Fat.* 24–5). For example, let us suppose that I am diagnosed with early-stage skin cancer and seek treatment. This action has a cause: me, and my deciding to seek the treatment. But that I engaged in that action was not itself causally necessitated; instead, it was entirely up to me.[8] But if we have such a power to engage in voluntary action, actions that are under our control in this strong sense, there is no reason to posit, in addition, a fundamental physical indeterminism like the swerve.[9]

Stoic criticisms of Epicurus

Chrysippus (*c.*280–206 BCE), the third head of the Stoic school, attacks Epicurus from the opposite direction in his reply to the lazy argument. He shows that causal determinism does not make the future inevitable in a manner that renders action or deliberation futile (*Fat.* 30). The Stoics believe that every event is both causally determined and fated. Every event occurs in accordance with god's providential plan, because god sets up the causal structure of the cosmos so that events unwind exactly as ordained in his plan. The Stoics wish to show that such a thoroughgoing determinism is compatible with human agency.

Let us return to my skin cancer. Chrysippus says that certain events are "co-fated": for instance, it is fated (and causally determined) *both* that I will recover from the cancer *and* that I will seek treatment; it is through my fated action of seeking treatment that my fated recovery will occur (*Fat.* 30). So if I am stricken by a skin cancer, and it is causally determined that I will not die as a result of the cancer, it does not follow that going to the doctor to get the cancer treated is pointless, since it is my action of going to the doctor and getting it treated that will bring about my recovery, instead of having the untreated melanoma metastasize and kill me. All that is needed for actions to have a point is that they be causally efficacious, so that statements of the following sort are true: "If you seek treatment, you will not be killed by the melanoma, and if you do not, you will be killed".

For many of our actions, I think that we can believe that what we are going to do is causally determined, and we can even know *what* action we will take (so "self-foreknowledge" is not a bar to acting), without rendering that action pointless or our deciding to act as we do irrational. For instance, if I am diagnosed with cancer and am told of the treatment options, I may perfectly well know exactly what I am going to do (I will get it removed), and I may believe that this action of mine is causally determined by my brain states that realize my beliefs about the cancer, my desire not to die young and so on. None of this would have any impact on the rationality of seeking treatment.

So if Chrysippus is right, it seems that Epicurus had no reason to fear determinism, and no reason to posit the swerve. He could have happily accepted Democritus' view that new motion always arises out of old, in an endless chain of causation, and that what will occur has already been set for ages, without needing to deny that what we do as agents has an impact on the world.

PART II

Epistemology: introduction and overview

Can we gain knowledge of the world? And if so, how do we gain knowledge of the world? These are two of the central questions asked in the branch of philosophy currently called "epistemology", or the theory of knowledge. The Epicureans themselves call this part of their philosophy "canonic", derived from the Greek word *kanōn*, or yardstick, and it is concerned with setting out the criteria of truth. The Epicureans are resolutely empiricist, with all of our concepts and knowledge ultimately being derived from the senses. Since the simple observation that there are bodies in motion serves as the linchpin of their physics, they must secure the reliability of the senses against sceptical attack. They do so, trying to show that scepticism is self-refuting. But scepticism is not merely theoretically unpalatable, it is *unliveable* (Chapter 9).

The three criteria of truth are sensations, "preconceptions" and feeling (*DL* X 31). The Epicureans set out their "canonic" with their physics (*DL* X 30). And for good reason: Epicurean epistemology is closely related to their psychology, which they understand as a branch of physics, the study of nature. They give an analysis of sensation as a purely passive reception of impressions from the environment, and they make the startling claim that all of these sensations are true. Repeated sensations give rise to "preconceptions", or basic concepts, and further concepts are generated by psychological operations on these basic concepts. With these two criteria, we are able to confirm or disconfirm particular judgements about the world as well as physical theories (Chapter 10).

Since feelings of pleasure and pain are the criteria of choice and avoidance (*DL* X 34), we shall deal with that part of the canon when we turn to Epicurean ethics.

NINE

Scepticism

A pattern of argument ubiquitous in Epicureanism is to start from something evident in sensation and on its basis infer a conclusion about realities hidden from direct observation. So, for example, Epicurus takes the obvious phenomenon of bodily motion to establish the existence of unobservable void. But predecessors of Epicurus such as Parmenides and Democritus, and successors of his, such as the Academic and Pyrrhonian Sceptics, marshalled powerful arguments against the reliability of the senses.

The Epicureans think that such a sceptical view of the senses is untenable. Before we look in Chapter 10 at the Epicureans' positive epistemology, we shall first examine their anti-sceptical arguments. That is because one of the primary Epicurean strategies for supporting their positive epistemology is to try to show that all other alternatives to their own views have untenable sceptical consequences. The Epicureans give three major anti-sceptical arguments. The first is that scepticism is self-refuting. The second is that the sceptic (*qua* sceptic) cannot have knowledge of the concepts needed to formulate the sceptical position. The third is that scepticism is unlivable.

Unfortunately, we do not have any extended Epicurean expositions of these arguments. However, Lucretius does briefly state each (*DRN* IV 469–99, IG I-27, LS 16A). Epicurus himself probably formulated these arguments against philosophers such as Parmenides and Democritus, who cast doubt on whether the senses were reliable. However, his younger compatriot Colotes extended the attack to Arcesilaus, who assumed the leadership of the Academy and turned it in a sceptical direction around the time of Epicurus' death. Arcesilaus argued that there are no sense-impressions that we cannot be mistaken about. As a result, we cannot gain knowledge, and we should suspend judgement. Centuries later, the Pyrrhonian Sceptic Sextus Empiricus asserted that the Academics were themselves dogmatists of a sort, in so far as they hold that knowledge is impossible, whereas the proper sceptic suspends judgement even on that question (*Pyr.* I 1-5, I 226). Both the Academic and Pyrrhonian Sceptics were well aware of the sorts of anti-sceptical arguments put forward by the Epicureans and responded to them. We shall look at these responses, in order to help highlight the philosophical issues raised by the Epicurean arguments.

The argument from self-refutation

The first argument is quite simple: if somebody thinks that nothing can be known, it follows from his position that he cannot know that nothing can be known. So there is no point in arguing with that person, as his position is self-refuting (*DRN* IV 469–72).

We need to be careful here. The *statement* "nothing can be known" is not self-contradictory, unlike the statement "this sentence is false". Lucretius' claim is that the *position* that nothing can be known cannot be consistently endorsed. If I am a dogmatist and claim that we can attain knowledge, and my sceptical interlocutor claims that I am wrong and states "I know that nothing can be known", he has immediately refuted himself. A sceptic putting his position forward for debate must immediately concede defeat, and in this sense his position is self-refuting.[1]

Any cautious sceptic, of course, will avoid claiming to know that he knows nothing, unless he enjoys paradox-mongering. One strategy for avoiding self-refutation, endorsed by the Academic Sceptic Cicero, softens the degree of commitment to the sceptical position.

Perhaps I cannot consistently *know* that knowledge is impossible. Still, I note the ways in which sensations often are deceptive, I take into account our inability to discover any reliable criterion for distinguishing true from false sensations, and I ponder the endless philosophical disputes over matters such as the existence of the gods and the good life for human beings. Given these facts, it is at least *plausible* to suppose that knowledge is impossible. And "it's plausible to suppose that knowledge is impossible" is not self-refuting (*Acad.* II 109–10). Still, Lucretius could try to reinstate his basic objection. If we gloss "it's plausible to suppose that *p*" as "I have good reason for believing *p*" or "I am justified in believing *p*", then Cicero's position becomes "I am justified in believing that knowledge is impossible". And then, as the statement "I am justified in believing that no beliefs are justified" *is* self-refuting, Lucretius could press the Academic Sceptic to spell out his grounds for thinking he can have justified beliefs while at the same time believing that knowledge is impossible.

The second sceptical strategy for avoiding self-refutation is quite different. The Pyrrhonian Sceptic Sextus Empiricus says that scepticism is not a doctrine, but a skill and a way of life (*Pyr.* I 8–11). The sceptic suspends judgement on all questions, including whether knowledge is possible. And because the sceptic has no sceptical doctrine, he does not have a self-refuting doctrine. Instead, what makes him a sceptic is that he has a knack for going around and producing suspension of judgement in himself and in others. So if I am an Epicurean he will present me with examples of apparent design in order to shake my confidence that the gods have nothing to do with the administration of the world and to cause me to have no opinion one way or the other on the topic, and likewise with my other pieces of self-assured dogma. He will have a toolbox of opposing arguments, many of them furnished by various dogmatic philosophers, ready at hand to whip out as need be. But these arguments are all dialectical – they are all aimed at *me*, proceeding from premises I accept or can be brought to accept – and the sceptic himself is not committed to any of their premises or conclusions.

This strategy seems to sidestep successfully the charge of self-refutation, although the Epicurean could try to claim that the sceptic has, at least implicitly, a sceptical position presupposed by his practice, one that can be dragged out into the light and examined for possible self-refutation. But as far as responding to the Pyrrhonian practice itself, the Epicurean would simply deal with the arguments as they come. For instance, they would argue that the putative pieces of godly beneficence, such as Socrates' observation in his version of the argument from design (Xen. *Mem.* 1.4.2–7) that the gods kindly put the anus far from the nose, give us little reason to believe in the existence of beneficent deities when weighed against the horrific suffering and manifest flaws in the world.

The argument from concept-formation

After giving the self-refutation argument, Lucretius states that the sceptic must also have knowledge in order even to formulate his position: knowledge of the meanings of his terms. In order to state "nothing can be known" and to give his arguments in support of the position, he will have to understand the meanings of terms such as "knowledge", "true", "false" and "doubtful" (*DRN* IV 473–7). So the act of stating the sceptical position demonstrates that it is false. And even in the case of the Pyrrhonian, who claims to have no position, Lucretius' argument could be applied: in engaging in his sceptical activity, the Pyrrhonian shows that he knows a great number of things, by his understanding of the terms of the arguments he proffers.

In theory, the sceptic strongly committed to the dialectical nature of his argumentative practice could reply that *he* does not claim to understand what he is talking about, that he is simply moving about the dogmatists' own terms in the way that they use them, and it is entirely on the dogmatist to make what he will of the sceptics' utterances. Prudently, Sextus does not go this route. Instead, he restricts the scope of his scepticism. The sceptic suspends judgement on the way things *are* in the world, and suspending judgement on these matters does not preclude him from making statements about how things *appear* to him (*Pyr.* I 13–15). In the case of concepts, the sceptic understands perfectly well what the Epicurean *means* by terms such as "body" and "atom", so he knows what the thesis "the mind is composed of atoms" *means*. But he suspends judgement on questions such as whether there *are* bodies and atoms in the world, and whether the mind is made of atoms or is incorporeal (*Pyr.* II 10–11).

Lucretius thinks, however, that the sceptic who casts doubt on the reliability of the senses cannot consistently avail himself of knowledge of concepts. As we shall see, the Epicureans have an empiricist account of concept-formation. For instance, I get basic concepts such as "cow" from having repeated sense-impressions of cows, caused by cows in my environment, and other non-basic concepts are formed by combining, augmenting and transposing these basic concepts. So, writes Lucretius, if scepticism were true – if we were unable to gain knowledge of the way the world is via our sensory interactions with the world – we would never have gained an understanding of concepts such as "true", as they have their origin in the senses (*DRN* IV 478–9). So in stating his position the sceptic shows us not only his knowledge of the meanings of his words but also the way in which our senses get us in touch with the world.

The sceptic would probably reject this argument as question-begging: Lucretius is already presupposing the reliability of the senses and that our basic concepts map onto the world, which is the very question at issue. Sextus writes that the sceptic "apprehends" the dogmatists' terms in the sense of understanding them, but he does not presuppose that these concepts arise from our senses interacting with that sort of object. Sextus adds that the dogmatist should not presuppose this either, as otherwise it would be impossible to enquire whether any X (e.g. god) exists without already presupposing that the object of your enquiry exists (*Pyr.* II 1–9).

The inaction argument

The final Epicurean objection to scepticism is the classic "inaction" (*apraxia*) argument, sometimes called the "lazy" argument. We saw earlier (Ch. 8, § "'Effective agency' and the pinciple of bivalence") how the Epicureans advance an argument of this sort against the principle of bivalence, asserting that to believe that truths about the future were settled since time immemorial would render action pointless. Similarly, scepticism would undercut the basis for any action. Lucretius writes that if you lose confidence in the trustworthiness of the senses, life would collapse, as you would have no reason to do things such as avoid cliffs and other hazards (*DRN* IV 500–510). After all, if the senses were unreliable, then the mere fact that it *looks as though* there is a cliff ahead would give me no reason to believe that there *is* a cliff ahead. And likewise, if the senses were unreliable, even if there *is* a cliff ahead, I would have no reason to suppose that if I walk off the cliff I shall fall down and dash my brains out on the rocks below, as that belief is founded on my observing that that is what has happened. The practical consequences of scepticism are illustrated by the amusing (although almost certainly apocryphal) stories told about the sceptic Pyrrho, after whom the Pyrrhonists named themselves, who was able to survive only because his friends were constantly pulling him back from cliff edges and out of the way of speeding carts (*DL* IX 62).

Initially, this argument appears invalid. After all, from the premise "believing *p* would make life unlivable", it does not follow that "*not-p*". At best, the argument would seem to show that scepticism regarding the senses is pragmatically unacceptable, not that it is false. We could try to make the argument valid by changing the premise slightly: people *are* able to use their senses to navigate around the world successfully and live their lives, and they would be unable to do so if the senses were unreliable. But put in this way, the argument appears question-begging: after all, we know that people can use their senses to navigate around the world successfully because we see that they do so. In any case, ancient sceptics did not question the *apraxia* argument in either of these ways, probably because ancient philosophies were supposed to be ways of life, not just theoretical positions. Instead, they try to show how one can live as a sceptic, so that scepticism does not have disastrous practical consequences.

The first sort of reply, once again, is offered by an Academic Sceptic. The sceptic who eschews claims of knowledge can still guide his life by the more modest criterion of the plausible. I may not *know* that there is a cliff ahead, that the door is a better way of exiting the classroom than the window, or that a peanut butter sandwich is a better meal than a handful of tacks, but all of these are highly plausible (*Acad.* II 103–4, LS 69I). Indeed, we need not confine ourselves to the plausibility of individual sense-impressions. The Academic Sceptic Carneades, from whom Cicero derives his notion of the "plausible" impression, devises an elaborate system for testing impressions. In important matters, we can investigate a plausible impression further and see whether it is corroborated by further impressions and whether it coheres with them. It *looks* like there is a snake ahead in the house, but further impressions could be of a snake or just a coiled rope, and a host of past impressions may help reinforce (or undercut) the plausibility of there being a snake in this house, in this climate (Sext. Emp. *Math.* VII 166–84, IG III-18, LS 69D–E).

The Epicurean would probably home in on the notion of "plausibility". Is "plausible" here no more than a measure of subjective convincingness? After all, the mere fact that something is highly plausible to me need not guarantee that it is true, a point that Carneades and Cicero themselves, as sceptics who eschew claims to knowledge, insist on. If so, then the plausibility of some impression gives me no reason to believe that it is true, that it reflects the way the world is, and then I have no reason to believe that acting on the basis of what is plausible is more likely to be successful than any other course of action. On the other hand, if sceptics believe that plausible impressions *are* more likely to be true than not, the Epicureans will ask what grounds the sceptic has, as a sceptic who believes knowledge is impossible, for this confidence.[2]

A different reply is offered by the founder of Academic Scepticism, Arcesilaus. This reply eschews even the weak sort of assent to something as plausible that Cicero and Carneades allow. The sceptic, says Arcesilaus, will still have sense-impressions: they arise in him involuntarily. So he will see the cliff in front of him. Likewise, he will have impulses to act. Instinctively, he will have an aversion to stepping off the cliff. These impressions and impulses will suffice for the sceptic to move around in the world, avoiding cliffs, stepping through doors and eating peanut butter sandwiches. The only thing that the sceptic avoids is assent. That is, the sceptic never decides to *believe* that there is a cliff in front of him, and likewise with the propositions that his other impressions furnish him. But he *should not* assent to these things, as doing so would be rash, and he *need not* assent to them, as impulses to act will arise anyway (Plut. *Adv. Col.* 1122a–f, IG III-12, LS 69A). Sextus Empiricus gives a similar account of how a sceptic can act. The sceptic has no beliefs about how things *are*. But the sceptic does not abolish the appearances, including sense-impressions and feelings. So it will still seem that there is a cliff in front of him, he will feel fear, it will look as if there is a peanut butter sandwich in front of him, it will seem tasty, he will feel hungry and so on. These impressions will move the sceptic around here and there without any beliefs (Sext. Emp. *Pyr.* I xi 21–4). So the sceptic has no criterion for belief, but he does have a criterion of action: the appearances.[3]

The Epicureans would probably have two objections here. The first is that the Arcesilean (and Sextan) reply implicitly assumes a faulty model of belief. Arcesilaus, for example, claims that he has no beliefs when he avoids the cliff and reaches for the sandwich. But Epicurus would say that Arcesilaus *does* really have beliefs, whatever he might say to the contrary, and that he has beliefs is evinced by his behaviour. Arcesilaus is assuming a Stoic model of cognition, not coincidentally, as the Stoics were the main dialectical opponents of the Academic sceptics. The Stoics sharply distinguish between human and animal action. Animals have involuntary impressions ("fire ahead") and the impulses that follow from them ("flee!"). For human beings, however, the process whereby impressions lead to impulses is mediated by assent. It is up to us whether to assent or not to the content of our impressions, and it is only when we assent that fully fledged beliefs are formed. For Arcesilaus, the sceptic can steer himself around as animals do without having the voluntary assents that lead to belief. But Epicurus would not make such a sharp divide between animal and human cognition. Animals have beliefs, as we do, and that some belief arises in us involuntarily and irresistibly does not mean that it is not really a belief.

Secondly, the Epicureans could repeat the point above about using the "plausible" as a criterion, if plausibility means merely subjective convincingness. Let us grant that animals act without thinking about whether or not their impressions are true. Nonetheless, their actions are effective because the senses of animals provide them with information about their environment. But the sceptic does not believe that the senses are reliable guides to the way the world is. So the sceptic seems to have no good justification for acting as he does.

TEN

The canon

The truth of all sensations

The first criterion of truth is sensation. But sceptics cast doubt on the veridicality of the senses, often by bringing up examples of conflicting appearances. The same wall that seems white to me will (supposedly) appear yellow to a man with jaundice. An oar seems bent when stuck partway under water but straight after being pulled out, and a tower seems round in the distance but square close up. The common-sense position is that some of these sensations are true, others false. Since the wall is really white, the oar really straight and the tower really square, the sensations that report these things are true, while the ones that report otherwise are false. But the sceptical response to this common-sense position is that we have no criterion to distinguish reliably between true and false sensations. And since we have no good way of deciding which sensations are true and which are false, we should suspend judgement.

Although Epicurus himself did not confront the sceptical challenge as formulated in precisely this way – it was put this way by later sceptics, the Academics and the Pyrrhonians – the general problem of conflicting appearances was featured prominently in earlier disputes about the reliability of the senses, and many people concluded on the basis of sensory variability that the senses could not be relied on. The Epicureans agree that if the truth of any sensation is cast into doubt, then there can be found no criterion whereby to distinguish the true from the false ones. Once we start to doubt the reliability of the senses, we cannot use reason to determine which sensations are true and which false, as reason itself is a product of sensation (*KD* 23, *DRN* IV 480–85). But as we saw in Chapter 9, the Epicureans regard such scepticism about the senses as self-refuting and unlivable. So they embrace the bold position that *all* sensations are true.

The position that all sensations are true appears to be itself obviously false. But Epicurus is willing to embrace its apparently absurd consequences, asserting that even the figments experienced by dreamers and madmen are true (*DL* X 32). The first move the Epicureans make in order to render this position at all plausible is to distinguish sharply between our sensations and the judgements about objects made on the basis of those sensations. When there is error, it enters in *always* in the "added opinion", that is, in the judgements we make about the world on the basis of our sensations (*Ep. Hdt.* 50). When we see a "bent" oar in the water, the sensation does not tell us *that* the oar itself is bent. The bent-shaped patch in our visual field is just the impression we are receiving from the oar, and *we* make a mistake when we infer that the oar itself is bent because of that impression. (In fact, with experience we learn that straight objects normally appear bent when partially stuck under the water, so we would be more likely to go wrong if the straight oar for some reason did *not* appear bent.) If the bent-oar example is unconvincing, we should conclude that the senses deceive us when they report that people far away are really tiny, but, of course, the senses report no such thing. As Lucretius puts it, it is the business of the mind to make such judgements (e.g. what size the people are) on the basis of the information the senses furnish, and so we should not blame the eyes for the mind's shortcomings (*DRN* IV 379–86).

Sensation does not make any judgements about the world. It just apprehends what is present to it, for example colour in the case of sight (Sext. Emp. *Math.* VII 210). One sense cannot refute another, because each has a different sort of object – colour for sight, sounds for hearing and so on – so their reports cannot conflict (*DL* X 32;

DRN IV 486–96). This insulates sensations from the possibility of error, but at the apparent cost of their not having any propositional content at all, of not saying *that* anything is the case. So it becomes quite murky the sense in which they are all true, as opposed to neither true nor false.

One way to make all sensations true is to restrict their propositional content to what is immediately given in the sensation itself, that is, that I am having a certain sort of visual, auditory, olfactory, gustatory or tactile experience. I may not know whether the wall is white, or the orange juice sweet. But that I am having a certain sort of sense-experience is obvious and cannot be denied, and this is all that the sensation itself is really saying. The Cyrenaics (a group of rival hedonists active shortly before and around the time of Epicurus) give a theory of this sort. They coin neologisms to make it clear that they are restricting themselves to just the sensation itself, saying that we can apprehend that "I am being whitened" when I (apparently) see the white wall, or that "I am being sweetened" when I (apparently) drink the sweet orange juice, because this content is self-evident and knowledge of it incorrigible (*Adv. Col.* 1120e; Sext. Emp. *Math.* VII 191).

But the Epicureans reject this position, even though they say that sensation as such is concerned only with what is immediately present to it, for example colour in the case of sight. The Epicurean Colotes mocks the Cyrenaics' neologisms, saying that the Cyrenaics refuse to admit that a horse exists, stating instead that they are horsed. But more seriously, if sensations inform us only of themselves, and we cannot use them to gain knowledge of the world, then we would be unable to act (*Adv. Col.* 1120d). The Epicureans have little interest in the supposedly immediate knowledge of one's own mental states; sensations are supposed to be one of the criteria whereby we can gain knowledge *of the world* and are thereby able to act effectively.

At this point, it is worth noting an ambiguity in the Epicurean slogan "all sensations are true". The Greek term I have been translating as "true", *alēthēs*, can also mean "real". And, in fact, many of the Epicurean discussions of the "truth" of all sensations point towards their using the term to mean that all sensations are real, not that they are true. Diogenes Laertius reports that our awareness proves that every sensation is *alēthēs* because it is as much a fact that we see and hear as that we feel pain. Our awareness of pain, colours and sounds may show that pain and sensations of colour and sound are *real*, but not that they are all *true*.

Another proof the Epicureans give for every sensation being *alēthēs* – including even the figments of madmen and dreamers – is that they all cause movement, whereas what does not exist does not move anything (*DL* X 32). Once again, this is a fine proof that sensations are real, but a bad one that they are true, and the obvious contradictory of "what does not exist" is "what does exist", not "what is true". So the Epicureans are not trying to say that the propositional contents of sensations are all true (as they have none), but simply that all sensations are real things. Sextus reports that even the sensations of Orestes, who saw the Furies pursuing him, were *alētheis* in so far as the images existed and moved his sensation; the error was in his mind when he concluded falsely that the Furies were solid bodies instead of phantasms (Sext. Emp. *Math.* XIII 63, LS 16F).

But this defence of the Epicurean position leads to a very different problem. Whereas the slogan "all sensations are true" seems absurd, the slogan "all sensations are real", that is, they exist, seems trivial and unhelpful. The Epicurean doctrine that every sensation is *alēthēs* is supposed to be a contribution to a debate about how we gain knowledge of the world and a response to scepticism. Responding to sceptical worries about the reliability of the senses by asserting "Yes, but sensations all exist" seems radically beside the point. The Epicureans need some way of avoiding both the Scylla of absurdity and the Charybdis of triviality.

The Epicureans do have such a way, as they do not think of sensations as purely private mental phenomena. Instead, they are effects of external causes. Objects in the environment throw off a continuous flow of "images" (*eidōla*) from their surfaces, and visual sensations result when these images bang into our eyeballs. Other sensations are also analysed as the result of atomic interactions between external objects and our sense-organs, for example the bitter taste of coffee is the result of barbed atoms tearing at our tongue. As such, sensations may not have propositional content in the way a statement or belief does, but they can still be *informative*. As Sextus Empiricus puts it, in reporting the Epicurean doctrine that every sensation is *alēthēs*, "every impression is the product of something existent and is *like the thing which moves the sense*" (*Math.* XIII 63). That is, not only are sensations effects, but we can reason from these effects about what sorts of things caused them.

So think of the images thrown off the surface of a square tower. A continuous series of them impacting our eyes gives us a visual sensation, like the impressions created on the stills of an old-fashioned movie camera as they absorb the light waves reflected off of the tower. The eye passively receives the impact of the images and records it. This sensation is "true" of the images in so far as the images are what (directly) move the sense, so that the sensation accurately reflects its shape. This shape will not be the same as the shape of the tower: the corners of the images are blunted as they pass through a great distance and are buffeted by the intervening air, so it looks roundish. But the image can still give us information regarding the tower, just as a photo can, even though the shape of the image on the film is not the same as the shape of the object itself.[1] After all, an object seen from a distance should not look the same as one seen close up.

Preconceptions

The second criterion of truth is "preconception", or *prolēpsis*. *Prolēpsis* is a technical term coined by Epicurus, and can also be translated "basic grasp". *Lēpsis* comes from the verb "to grasp", but it often is used to form words that have overtones of a *cognitive* grasp, so "basic cognition" would serve as a translation too.

Epicurus uses preconceptions to solve the celebrated paradox of enquiry, which Socrates puts forward in Plato's dialogue the *Meno* (*Men.* 80d–e). The paradox is supposed to show that enquiry is impossible. Let us suppose you are trying to learn something, such as what virtue is. Either you know what you are looking for, or you do not. If you already know it, there is no point in enquiring after it.

But if you do not already know what you are looking for, enquiry is impossible, as you would not be able to recognize the correct answer even if you were to come across it. In response to this paradox, Socrates develops the theory that all "learning" is really recollection. You already know what you are enquiring after, but only implicitly. When you discover truth you recognize it, fully remembering what you had half-forgotten. This innate knowledge that makes enquiry possible, Socrates asserts, must have existed in our souls in a prenatal existence, with the shock of being embodied causing our souls to have amnesia.

Epicurus opts for a more economical solution. He agrees that enquiry requires previous knowledge; for example, I cannot ask "Is that thing over there a horse or a cow?" unless I already know what a horse and a cow are (*DL* X 33). And when it comes to the definitions of words, not all words must require definition in terms of other words, on pain of an infinite regress. Instead, the meanings of some words we simply grasp without need of additional proof (*Ep. Hdt.* 37–8). When we have repeated sense-experiences of the same sort of thing, this gives us a memory of what has often appeared, and this memory is the universal idea or preconception. When the word associated with that concept is uttered, we call up the memory; for example, when somebody says "human being", I immediately have a general outline of a human being and think "that sort of a thing is a human being" (*DL* X 33). We may enquire further about the features human beings have in common that make them human beings, but that is not the meaning of "human being". Instead, "human being" simply picks out those sorts of things over there, those things I have seen around all over the place. As with the instinctive animal utterances that form the basis of human language (see Ch. 6, § "Language"), the meanings of preconceptions are set by the sorts of items that cause them.

Once we have preconceptions, further ideas are formed by analogy or by similarity or by compounding these basic ideas. But since preconceptions themselves are formed by our experiences, ultimately all of our ideas are based on our experiences. Whatever questions may be raised about this, the basic idea seems fairly straightforward for many of our preconceptions, such as "human being" and "body". But included among our preconceptions are usefulness (*DRN* IV 853–7), truth (*DRN* IV 473–9), god (which we shall look at in Chapter 16) and our own agency, where the supposed empirical basis is much less obvious. Unfortunately, we do not have explanations of how most of these preconceptions arise.

But a discussion of how we come to have the preconception of our own agency has been preserved. Some things happen of necessity, whereas others depend on us and are our own responsibility. Our preconceptions of necessity and of our own responsibility arise by observing ourselves in action, as we deliberate among options, advise one another and admonish one another. We see that sometimes we can do things we do not want to (e.g. submitting to a root canal treatment now to avoid greater pain later), and that we can dissuade others from doing something they are considering only because they are being threatened (e.g. convincing someone not to betray his friend despite the prospect of the rack). It is from these observations that we get the idea that some things are of necessity while others depend on us. We show our awareness of the distinction in our interactions: we try to dissuade others from actions that "depend on us", those that are under our rational control, which would be pointless for those that are of necessity. So our idea of our own agency does have an empirical basis, albeit one that is not as straightforward as the empirical basis of the idea "cow".[2]

Confirmation and multiple explanations

Sensations form the first and primary part of the canon, the yardstick whereby we decide what is the case. Every one of them gives us some information about the world. But this obviously leaves open the question of how we go from this information to make judgements about objects, as sensations themselves do not do this. Once repeated sense-experiences have formed preconceptions in us (and we develop further ideas formed via operations on these basic ideas), we can make judgements about the world, framed in terms of these concepts, based on the information we receive through our senses. We do not just get some colour and shape in our visual field, we think "Oh, maybe there is a round tower over there". As we have noted, this stage is where error arises.

The Epicurean account of how we can make accurate judgements about the world regarding day-to-day empirical matters is surprisingly humdrum. We form a preliminary opinion about something based on our sensation: for example, "Plato is over there" or "that tower is round". This conjectural opinion still awaits confirmation, and whether it turns out to be true or false depends on further testimony from the senses, to see whether the object of opinion is as I believed it to be: for example, I see Plato close up and it is obvious that it is Plato; or I approach the tower, and close up it is clear that I was wrong, as the tower is actually square (*DL* X 34; Sext. Emp. *Math.* VII 211–12). So these clear, obvious observations, which allow us to confirm and disconfirm our opinions, are the basis of everything (Sext. Emp. *Math.* VII 216).

But at this point, it looks as though the sceptic can reinstate his challenge. The Epicureans insulate sensations from the possibility of error by sharply distinguishing sensations themselves and the judgements made on their basis. But what criterion will we use to distinguish true from false opinions? Simply to reply blandly that we confirm or disconfirm opinions on the basis of further observations, as the Epicureans do, will not work, because the judgements based on those further observations are themselves always liable to error. For instance, I see somebody in the distance and think, "Hmm, looks like Plato". Then I approach him and, seeing his distinctive and wonderful physiognomy up close, I think, "Aha! Yes indeed, clearly that's Plato". But unknown to me, Plato has an evil twin brother Schmato, who recently disposed of Plato and is impersonating him as head of the Academy.[3] The Academic Sceptics raised these sorts of objections against the Stoics, and the two schools had a long and fruitful exchange regarding them. But we do not have any record of how the Epicureans responded, if they did at all.

The Epicurean account of the confirmation of physical theories is a little more complicated. The Epicureans think that the basic principles of their system are entailed by the phenomena, as only these hypotheses are (supposedly) consistent with phenomena such as compound bodies moving around. Without void, there would be no motion, but that there are bodies in motion is obvious. Likewise, spatial minima are necessary for motion. Without the swerve, there would be no compound bodies, but that there are compound bodies is obvious. Even in these cases, however, the Epicureans do try to show that their hypotheses are at least possible: for example, by showing that the notion of absolutely empty space is coherent by analogizing it with the "empty" space in our experience and that the notion of an absolutely smallest spatial minimum is coherent by analogizing it with a minimum in our visual field.

The situation is quite different when it comes to the explanations of cosmological and meteorological phenomena, such as eclipses. We can be absolutely confident that they do not occur because of the wills of the gods, and that the heavenly bodies themselves are not divine, as these are inconsistent with the blessedness of the gods. That is fortunate, because having this knowledge is crucial for attaining a blessed life (*Ep. Hdt.* 76–8). But once we have excluded divine purpose, knowing the precise explanation of these phenomena in atomic terms does not much matter, as long as we know that there is *some* such explanation.

So the Epicureans are content to go through these phenomena and list bunches of possible explanations, saying that it could be caused by A, or B, or C, and so on (*Ep. Pyth.* 92–115; *DRN* V 592–770). This reticence is partly due to an admirable intellectual humility. Epicurus says that a person who insists on accepting one theory while others are equally consistent with the phenomena has blundered from physics into mythology (*Ep. Pyth.* 87). Lucretius draws an analogy with seeing a dead body in the distance. We should list all of the possible causes of death – cold, disease, poison and so on – and we can be confident that his death has some physical cause. But we should not presume to know which one in particular caused his death without more information (*DRN* VI 703–11). But it also reflects a deep incuriosity. The *only* purpose served by knowing the causes of cosmological and meteorological phenomena is securing freedom from disturbance. So once we have some plausible-sounding possible naturalistic explanations of the phenomena that do not invoke the gods, that is good enough, and there is no point in trying to find out which explanation is the actual one (*Ep. Hdt.* 79–80; *Ep. Pyth.* 85–8). Of course, given the infinity of time and space, if some phenomenon admits of multiple explanations (that are physically and not merely epistemically possible), then each of those explanations *will* be the correct explanation in some world, if not in ours (*DRN* V 526–33; LS 18D).

PART III

Ethics: introduction and overview

Epicurean ethics does not follow directly from their metaphysics and epistemology, but it has close connections to both. For almost all Greek philosophers of the time, the fundamental questions of ethics were (i) what is the highest good and (ii) how do you attain it, with the highest good being what is desirable for its own sake and not for the sake of anything else. Epicurus declares pleasure to be the highest good. In a world without purpose and plan, we can still observe the behaviour of animals and see that all of them (including human beings) pursue only pleasure for its own sake and likewise shun pain, establishing the intrinsic desirability of pleasure and badness of pain. The goodness of pleasure and badness of pain are also supposed to be evident in our experience (Chapter 11).

From this simple starting-point, however, Epicurus quickly develops a distinctive version of hedonism by asserting that mental pleasures and pains are greater than mere bodily pleasures and pains. Furthermore, lack of bodily pain and freedom from mental turmoil are not neutral states, but themselves pleasurable: indeed, the highest sorts of pleasures. So Epicurean hedonism turns out to be the pursuit of tranquillity, attained primarily by shedding the vain and empty desires that lead to anxiety and by leading a moderately ascetic life (Chapter 12).

Mainstream Greek ethics also stresses the central place of developing the virtues – excellences of character and thought – in attaining a happy life, and Epicurus is no exception. Epicurean hedonism is an *enlightened* hedonism, which recognizes that one must be brave, temperate and wise in order to live pleasantly. But Epicurus is unusual in insisting that the virtues are only *instrumental* goods, good only for the sake of the pleasure they produce, instead of being good for their own sake. Likewise, philosophy itself is needed to attain pleasure, but has no intrinsic value (Chapter 13).

Epicurus also wishes to include prominent places for justice and friendship in his hedonism. He develops an original version of a social contract theory of justice. Justice is a human artefact, created by our agreements about how to behave in our communities, but an artefact that is natural for us to create. Because the purpose of justice is to help members of the community live free from trouble, laws that are not useful for fulfilling this purpose are not just. The wise Epicurean recognizes the usefulness of justice for everybody and has no reason to behave unjustly (Chapter 14). Friendship is even more important for happiness. More than anything else, knowing that you have a network of friends you can rely on to look after you when you are in need gives you peace of mind. But in order to develop such friendships, you must be absolutely trustworthy as a friend yourself, helping out your friends when they are in need, even when it causes you great troubles. Indeed, the Epicureans say some things about friendship that appear to conflict with their egoist hedonism (i.e. their view that what one desires for its own sake is *one's own* pleasure): for instance, that the wise man will love his friend as much as himself and will be willing to die for his friend (Chapter 15).

Epicurean physics is largely devoted to dispelling any traces of divine influence from the workings of the world, because fear of the gods is one of the main impediments to happiness. However, Epicurus does not concede that denying that the gods have anything to do with our world makes him impious or an atheist. It is the opinions of the many, of gods meddling with the world, that are impious and that cause turmoil. Instead, true reverence consists in worshipping gods who are ideals of the most blessed life, a blissful life free of anger, jealousy or trouble (Chapter 16). The other great fear that Epicureanism promises us liberation from is the fear of death. Once we realize that death is annihilation, we should also realize that, as simply an eternity of nothingness, death cannot be bad for us, as we no longer exist to be harmed. And with nothing to fear in death, we can concentrate our energies where we should, on attaining blessedness here and now, in the only life we have (Chapter 17).

ELEVEN

Pleasure, the highest good

Teleological ethics in a non-teleological world

Epicurus' ethics operates within the framework articulated by Aristotle, a framework that systematizes the ethical thinking of Aristotle's predecessors and was accepted by almost all later Greek philosophers.[1] The central question of ethics is: what is the highest good? The good of something is its *telos*, its goal or purpose. This teleological analysis of the good extends quite widely; we can ask what the good is, not only of human life, but also of actions, artefacts, crafts such as medicine and so on. And in each case, we discover the item's good by discovering its goal or purpose.

But some goods are instrumental goods, that is, goods desired for the sake of some further good. I may go to the medicine cabinet in order to take some nasty cherry-flavoured cough syrup. So taking the cough syrup is the goal, and the good, of that action. But the nasty cough syrup is not desired for its own sake; instead, I pursue it in order to quell my awful hacking. Aristotle says that the highest good must be an intrinsic good and not an instrumental good: something that is desired only for its own sake and not for the sake of something else.

Aristotle believes that there are a multiplicity of intrinsic goods, such as pleasure, honour, virtue and friendship, each of which is worth pursuing for its own sake even if no other benefit results.

However, each of them is pursued also because we think that by obtaining them we will help make our lives happy, and we do not pursue happiness for the sake of something else. So Aristotle proclaims happiness as the highest good. "Happiness" (*eudaimonia*) is not a matter of having an elevated mood at some moment ("I was happy when I heard that George Michael was finally releasing his album of Abba covers"), but of one's life as a whole going well.

Epicurus accepts Aristotle's teleological analysis of the good, his contention that the highest good is what is sought for its own sake and not for the sake of anything else, his designation of happiness as the highest good and his idea that happiness is a matter of one's life, considered as a whole, going well. But this may seem incongruous. After all, one of Epicurus' main goals in his physics is to expel teleological explanations of natural phenomena, including the sorts of teleological explanations of biological phenomena favoured by Aristotle. For Aristotle, the eyes have a purpose (seeing) no less than does a knife (cutting), so that we can say that eyes fulfil their purpose when they see well. Likewise, our reason has a purpose (attaining the truth). And since reason is the highest part of human beings, the happiest life – that is, one that best fulfils the purpose inherent in our nature as human beings – will largely consist of reasoning well, and acting in ways that are rational.[2] (In particular, it will largely consist of contemplating the truths of theology and ontology.) Epicurus would reject all this argument. Human beings, and their organs, have no inherent purpose. Our minds were not made in order to think, and our hands were not made to grasp, even though our minds can think well and our hands can grasp well, and we can use our minds and hands to get what we wish. Each is useful, but not designed, unlike artefacts.

However, even though animals may have no *purpose*, they still have *purposes*. That is, they have desires and strive to attain the objects of those desires. So we do not need to discern our inherent *telos* in order to discover the purpose of life. Instead, in order to find the highest good we simply have to observe what, as a matter of fact, people desire and pursue for its own sake and not for the sake of anything else.

So Epicurus accepts Plato's thesis that the good is the ultimate object of desire, but with a twist. For Plato, we desire what is good because it is good, whereas for Epicurus, pleasure is the good because we desire it. Furthermore, Epicurus would reject the notion of a Form of the Good whereby all good things are good, and not only for the obvious reason that it is a metaphysical extravagance inconsistent with materialism. Epicureans think that the whole notion of something being good *per se* (which the Form of the Good is supposed to be above all else) is a category mistake. Just like "healthy", "good" is a relational property. Peanut butter is healthy for me, although it would be deadly for my son with the peanut allergy, and it cannot be healthy *as such*, without filling in *for which organism* or other it is healthy. And my pleasure is good for me, although it is probably indifferent for George Bush, and it cannot be "good" as such, without filling in *for which agent* it is good.

Epicurus' arguments for psychological hedonism

The Epicureans give two arguments to try to establish the thesis of psychological egoistic hedonism: the thesis that the only thing we desire for its own sake is our own pleasure (Cic. *Fin.* I 30).[3] The first is usually dubbed the *cradle argument*. The easiest and clearest case to look at in order to find what ultimately drives us all is the behaviour of infants, who clearly obey the pleasure principle. A baby feels the pangs of hunger and cries out. She is picked up and sees the bottle nearby. She eagerly latches on and sucks, feeling the gratification of the milk rolling over her tongue, sliding down her throat and quieting her pangs, until she is content. It is worth noting that the infant is pursuing *her own* pleasure and shunning *her own* pain.

The second argument we may dub the *argument from immediate experience*. The goodness of pleasure and badness of pain are simply supposed to be obvious in our experience of them. Are you really wondering whether pleasure is good? Well, then think of some pleasure, for example the pleasure of receiving a really good shoulder rub after a long and stressful day. The goodness of this pleasure is evident in our experience of it, just as is the heat of a nearby fire. In neither case is any long argument required; one simply needs to point out what is the case (Cic. *Fin.* I 30). Likewise, if you were curious about whether pain is bad, a swift kick to the shin (followed by the question "Was that bad?") should quell your doubts.[4]

We can derive ethical conclusions from psychological premises. Once psychological egoistic hedonism has been established, on this basis the Epicureans infer ethical egoistic hedonism: that the only thing that is intrinsically valuable is our own pleasure. This inference can be challenged by questioning either its validity or the truth of its premise.

Many people influenced by Immanuel Kant (and others besides) may assert that it does not follow from the mere fact that we all *desire* pleasure that we *ought to* desire pleasure. As a matter of fact, we desire many things we ought not to desire, and the ethically relevant question is not what we do desire, but what we ought to. But Epicurus (once he puzzled out what was meant by "ought" here) would probably not be very impressed by this challenge and side with John Stuart Mill against Kant that the only way to establish what the *desirable* is is to see what people, as a matter of fact, desire, and that there is no other sense of "desirable" apart from this that is relevant for deciding what to choose and avoid.[5]

Epicurus does believe that we desire many things we ought not to, and that there are many pleasures we ought not to pursue. However, these determinations can be made only after it has been established, by looking at what we ultimately desire, that pleasure is the highest good. Given that pleasure is the highest good, we can criticize my son's desire to play with matches by saying that, even though it is fun, it will lead to painful burns and possibly skin grafts, so that he will not be getting what he ultimately wants. Likewise, says Epicurus, all pleasures are good, but not all are choiceworthy, and all pains bad, but not all such as to be avoided. That is because some pleasures lead to more pain in the long run, and vice versa, so we have to think about the long-term consequences when choosing among pleasures and pains to make sure that we make our life overall as pleasant as we can (*Ep. Men.* 129–30). The pleasure of shooting up heroin is good, but not worth choosing, and the pain of getting an abscessed tooth drilled is bad but worth undergoing.

But it is far from obvious that the one thing we desire for its own sake is our own pleasure. The Stoics argue directly against the Epicurean cradle argument, offering an alternative explanation of infant behaviour. An infant's first impulse is towards not pleasure but self-preservation. An infant has an instinctive awareness of its own bodily constitution and what is natural to it. So the hungry infant is not seeking pleasure. Instead, she is aware of the disruption of hunger and wishes to get milk in order to restore herself to a full, healthy state. And as they develop, babies have an instinctive awareness of the proper use of their limbs and other bodily parts, and they wish to use them and develop them, even when it causes pain. Seneca gives the example of an infant struggling to stand up (presumably, just to do so, and not to get food or the like), who persists in the effort, even through repeated falls and tears (Sen. *Ep.* 121.6–15, LS 57B; see also *DL* 7.85–6, LS 57A).

Aristotle would attack the whole procedure of looking at infants to find out what people ultimately desire. After all, infants are immature members of the species, and as such should not be used to find out what human beings desire by nature. Infants are limited, with a limited range of desires, and we should look to fully functioning adults to find out what human beings naturally strive for. And adults strive for a much wider range of things than merely their own pleasure: things such as their friends' welfare, honour and knowledge of the workings of the cosmos. All human beings by nature desire to know (*Metaph.* I 1), but this desire is not yet evident in infants.

Epicurus would reply that the real root cause of our behaviour is easiest to see in infants, whose following of the desire for pleasure is relatively uncomplicated. Adults have much more complicated belief structures, so telling what is motivating them is more difficult. Furthermore, they often have been corrupted by society, learning to desire pointless things in the false belief that getting them will bring pleasure. ("I want that Botox injection because it will make me so much prettier, and then people will finally like me more!") Even in these complicated, corrupted cases, however, the same basic natural desires present in infants are also fuelling our behaviour.

TWELVE

Varieties of pleasure, varieties of desire

Because the Epicureans proclaim that pleasure is the highest good, they have often been tarred with the same brush that tars all hedonists: that they are unscrupulous, unbridled sensualists, busy stuffing themselves with dainties from the local Epicurean shop before engaging in lascivious dances and disgusting orgies. The Epicureans rightly protest that this involves a gross misunderstanding of their philosophy. Instead, mental pleasures are greater than physical pleasures, and lack of pain is itself a kind of pleasure. Indeed, the highest sort of pleasure is tranquillity, freedom from fear and anxiety. So they recommend paring down one's desires to only the natural and necessary ones, which are easy to satisfy, and thereby gaining self-sufficiency and the confidence regarding the future that accompanies it.

Varieties of pleasure

The first distinction Epicurus makes is between mental and bodily pleasures and pains. In some sense, of course, *all* pleasures and pains are mental, in so far as one has to have a mind in order to experience them, and one experiences them primarily with one's mind (although the Epicureans insist that the body too has a share in sensation). Likewise, in some sense all pleasures and pains are bodily, in so far as animals and their minds are corporeal, and pleasures and pains are (in this sense) corporeal states. Still, there are some pleasures and pains that are bodily in a commonsensical way. When I am hungry, or my hand is smashed with a meat tenderizer, I am aware of something wrong with my bodily state right now. And when I am enjoying the taste of a banana, or the sensation of a good shoulder rub, I am aware of something good going on with my body right now.

Mental pleasures and pains, unlike bodily pleasures and pains, are not confined to the present, but span the past, present and future. Memories of past painful experiences can themselves be painful, and memories of pleasurable ones pleasurable. Recalling being humiliated at school can still be painful today, whereas thinking back to hiking the mountains of Samos is soothing. Indeed, the Epicureans recommend that people should train themselves to recall sweet memories as a way to have pleasure always available to them (Cic. *Fin*. I 57). Epicurus himself apparently did this while dying. He claimed that he was able to endure with equanimity the terrible agony of kidney stones by recalling past philosophical conversations with a friend (*DL* X 22). Likewise, anticipating the future can be painful or pleasurable, depending on how I expect it to go. If I have to go to get my wisdom tooth extracted by an incompetent dentist who performed the procedure badly the previous time, my anxiety in the week leading up to the procedure may well cause me more suffering than the operation itself. But if I manage to find another dentist recommended by friends, who in addition will do the procedure under full anaesthetic, I will face the procedure with a feeling of sweet serenity. These sorts of mental pleasures and pains, although they *depend* on bodily pleasures and pains – ultimately, they involve memories of past bodily pleasures and pains or anticipations of future bodily pleasures and pains – are nonetheless greater (Cic. *Fin.* I 55).

The Cyrenaics, a group of rival hedonists who flourished around the time of Epicurus, disagree on both counts. First, they claim that bodily pains are worse than mental ones – presumably on the ground that they are, on the whole, more vivid and intense – and adduce as evidence for this that we punish wrongdoers with bodily pain (*DL* X 137). As noted, Epicurus disagrees with this on the grounds that mental pains encompass past, present and future, while bodily ones are confined to the present. But he could also have noted that, if we equate happiness with a pleasant life and unhappiness with a painful one (as hedonists should), most extremely unhappy people are unhappy not because they have a greater amount of bodily pains than others, but because of feelings of regret, dissatisfaction, anxiety and fear. And exceptionally happy people do not typically outstrip the rest of us in having more bodily pleasures, but greater joy and tranquillity.

But the Cyrenaics seem to have a stronger point when they object that not all mental pleasures depend on bodily ones. They give the examples of taking joy in conversations and ambitions (presumably, the memory of conversations and the anticipation of fulfilling one's ambitions). Indeed, Epicurus himself seems to be describing exactly such a pleasure in the letter he dictates while in physical agony on the last day of his life, and Lucretius also describes his awe at beholding the wondrous workings of the universe, as revealed by Epicurus (*DL* X 22; *DRN* III 28–30). Basing all mental pleasures and pains on bodily ones is far too restrictive. The Epicureans could try to reply by saying that mental pleasures and pains need not each *directly* depend on bodily pleasures and pains, but only *indirectly*. For example, the ambition for political office may itself be held because a person (mistakenly) believes that by securing it he will be able to gain security from attacks by other people and enrich himself so as to satisfy his urge for bodily pleasures, and then my anticipation that I will attain this office is pleasurable. Still, such a manoeuvre probably covers at best only some mental pleasures and pains.

The second distinction Epicurus makes is between kinetic and katastematic pleasures. "Kinetic" pleasures, as the name suggests, involve movement. Bodily kinetic pleasures are associated with some sort of active titillation of the senses, for example the savoury, greasy taste of a sausage slathered with mustard as it caresses my tongue. They also seem to be associated with the *process* of satisfying some desire. For example, I am hungry, and this hunger is painful. But then, as I chew the sausage and swallow it, I am in the process of satisfying my desire for food and replenishing myself, and this process would be a bodily kinetic pleasure. These kinetic pleasures are what we usually think of when we think of pleasure.

But now, think of my state after I have eaten the sausage. I am full, and no longer suffering from the pain of hunger. The key Epicurean innovation is to insist that this state – of not being in pain or need, of having one's desires satisfied – is *not* merely a neutral state, but another type of pleasure, a "katastematic" pleasure. The simple principle that allows us to declare such states pleasures is that everything we take delight in is a pleasure, just as everything that distresses us is a pain (Cic. *Fin.* I 37). And we take delight not only in sensory titillation, but also in the state of being free from pain or want.

On the mental side, Epicurus classifies "joy" as a kinetic pleasure (*DL* X 137). And the mental katastematic pleasure of being free from regret, fear and anxiety is *ataraxia*, or tranquillity.

Not only does Epicurus insist that these "katastematic" pleasures are pleasures, but he classifies them as the greater sort of pleasure. Indeed, he says that the removal of all pain is the limit of pleasure (*KD* 3), and that once this limit is reached, pleasure cannot be increased but only varied (*KD* 18). This is why he says, "The cry of the flesh: not to be hungry, not to be thirsty, not to be cold. For if someone has these things and is confident of having them in the future, he might contend even with Zeus for happiness" (*SV* 33, trans. in IG). A full, hydrated and comfortably warm person has reached the limit of bodily pleasure, which is *aponia*, or freedom from bodily distress. And since mental pleasures and pains depend on bodily pleasures and pains, a person who has confidence that he will continue on in this comfortable state will reach the limit of mental pleasure, which is *ataraxia*, or tranquillity. And this combination of *aponia* and *ataraxia* – with *ataraxia* being by far the more important of the two – is the pinnacle of happiness. Epicurus is properly called a hedonist, since he avows that pleasure is the sole intrinsic good. But given his idiosyncratic understanding of pleasure, with *ataraxia* being the primary constituent of the happy life, it may be less misleading to call him a "tranquillist".

Understandably, this theory of pleasure attracted a wide range of attacks. The Cyrenaics claim that, for Epicurus, the happiest person is a corpse or somebody asleep (*DL* 2 88 [IG I-10]; Clement of Alexandria *Stromates* 2.21,130.8–9 [IG I-13]). But the Epicureans seem to have a ready reply. While corpses are free from pain and anxiety, there is a large difference between being unconscious and being tranquil. Corpses do not take delight in being free from fear, while we can. So the Epicureans could say, quite reasonably, that while *aponia* and *ataraxia* are defined negatively as freedom from bodily and mental pain, they are still positive mental states that require a person to be aware of them to be pleasures.

Cicero raises a more serious set of objections (Cic. *Fin.* II 28–35). First, he claims that the lack of pain is not properly called a pleasure. We all understand pleasure to involve some sort of "sweet sensation", as do those pleasures that Epicurus calls "kinetic". If Epicurus wishes to say that the absence of pain is also intrinsically good, he may do so. But he should not ineptly group two disparate phenomena with little in common – pleasure and the absence of pain – under the single label of "pleasure". Instead, he should just admit that we have a composite highest good: attaining both pleasure and the absence of pain. Or, since Epicurus misleadingly speaks of the absence of pain as the "limit of pleasure", even though at other times he extols the pleasures of the senses, perhaps he would be better off simply admitting that the highest good is the absence of pain.[1]

But this admission would expose Epicurus to Cicero's second objection. In his proof of hedonism, Epicurus points to the behaviour of infants. But, says Cicero, Epicurus believes that what rouses infants to action is the prospect of sensory pleasures, that is, "kinetic" pleasures, not merely the so-called pleasure of absence of pain. So, in order to remain consistent with the starting-point of his ethics, he should have said that kinetic pleasure is the highest good. But, embarrassed to expound such a sensualist theory, Epicurus switched to praising the austere, respectable "katastematic" pleasures instead. Although initially plausible, Cicero's appeal to infant behaviour is not decisive against the Epicurean theory. Babies can be motivated by the prospects of a clean nappy, a full tummy and a warm blanket. And having attained all these things, they enjoy their state and are utterly content, needing nothing more to add to their pleasure.

Still, the first objection remains. Epicurus could simply and blandly repeat the formula that "anything we take delight in is a pleasure", which encompasses both kinetic and katastematic pleasures and is sufficient to unite them as a single class. But this reply may seem insufficient. Furthermore, it leaves unanswered the questions of why katastematic pleasures are the greatest pleasures and why, once the state of freedom from pain has been attained, pleasure can be "varied" but not increased. Imagine that I am enjoying the state of being hydrated, full and warm. Then somebody offers me a small chocolate bon-bon, and I greatly enjoy the delicious taste of the dark chocolate. Why am I not experiencing more pleasure now than I was before, with the bon-bon pleasure added on top of all those katastematic pleasures? More generally, what is the place of kinetic pleasures (which the Epicureans admit are intrinsically good) in the Epicurean theory of the highest good, which seems to exclude them in preference to the katastematic pleasures of *aponia* and *ataraxia*?

These sorts of puzzles and difficulties have led some to think that perhaps Cicero slightly misunderstands or misrepresents the root of the Epicurean distinction between the two types of pleasure.[2] (Cicero's description of the distinction, our fullest report of it, has been the basis for the explanation of it above.) On this interpretation, Epicurus' thinking on pleasure takes as its starting-point Plato's discussion of pleasure and pain in the *Philebus*. According to Socrates, pain is the perceived disruption to or dissolution of an organism's natural, healthy state. Pleasure is the perceived process of restoration of the organism toward its natural, healthy state (*Phlb.* 42d). This theory fits in with Lucretius' descriptions of hunger, thirst, pain and pleasure. Lucretius writes that the substance of creatures' bodies inevitably suffers losses over time as they exert themselves, undermining their bodily constitution. Awareness of this causes gaping hunger and panting thirst, and creatures instinctively seek food and water in order to restore their bodies and satisfy these cravings

(*DRN* IV 858–76). Likewise, Lucretius says that pain occurs when the particles of matter in the body are disturbed from their place and reel around, whereas pleasure occurs when they are returning to their position (*DRN* II 963–6).

However, Socrates also says that the state in which one's health is being neither restored nor disrupted is neither pleasurable nor painful (*Phlb.* 42d–e; see also *Rep.* 583c–584a), which implies that the state of having had one's health restored is not pleasurable, whereas Epicurus insists that being aware that one is healthy in body and mind is highly pleasurable. So what distinguishes kinetic and katastematic pleasures is that kinetic pleasures are ones we are aware of while in the *process* of replenishing ourselves and restoring our natural state, whereas katastematic pleasures are the ones we are aware of when we are in the *state* of functioning naturally and healthily. This natural, healthy state will be painless. But it will involve awareness and sensory pleasures, pleasures that (*contra* Cicero's report of Epicureanism in book one of *On Ends*) should be classified as katastematic, not kinetic.

On this view, Epicurus has perfectly good reason to set a limit on pleasure: once one has reached the state of functioning perfectly healthily in body and mind, a state that moreover is free of all turmoil and distress, one cannot increase the "amount" of that state or the satisfaction one takes in it. In this way, Epicurean pleasure would be almost utterly unlike Benthamite pleasure. For Jeremy Bentham, one can always toss another pleasure on top of the ones you are currently experiencing, or crank up the dial in the pleasure machine to increase the intensity of some pleasure from 10 to 11, and thereby increase the total number of hedons. Epicurus would also have some justification for his odd claim that unlimited and limited time contain equal amounts of pleasure (*KD* 19). For a Benthamite, duration increases amount: all else being equal, ten minutes of back rub pleasure will produce twice as many hedons as five minutes. But on the Epicurean view, it is far less clear that quantifying the amount of pleasure one receives according to how long it lasts makes any sense.

Varieties of desire

Epicurus, as noted above, advocates sorting through possible pleasures and pains and choosing among them based on their long-term consequences. The beer a friend is offering me now will bring me pleasure, and that pleasure is good. But because I have a job interview an hour hence, I should not choose this pleasure, as it would be more than outweighed by the pains caused by my not receiving the job and feeling great self-loathing. The main emphasis of Epicurean ethics, however, is not so much on picking and choosing from particular courses of action, as in the example above. Instead, it is on changing *ourselves*, by thinking through what we desire and making sure that we want only what we really need.

The Epicureans believe that to have a desire is to think we lack something good, which is painful, whereas the process of satisfying our desires, and especially the state of being free from want or need, are pleasant. So pleasure and desire-satisfaction are closely bound up. With respect to any given desire, we can take one of two strategies regarding it: we can strive to fulfil it, or we can eliminate it. For the most part, the Epicureans plump for the latter, advocating desire-reduction as the path to happiness.

The Epicureans divide desires into three classes: (i) natural and necessary; (ii) natural but not necessary; and (iii) vain and empty. Examples of natural and necessary desires are desires for food, drink and shelter. They are "natural" in the sense that all human beings naturally have them: we do not have to learn to want food when hungry, but seek it out instinctively. Because such desires are "hard-wired" in us in this way, they are difficult if not impossible to eliminate. Epicurus says they are "necessary" either for happiness, or in order to live free from bodily trouble, or even to live, period (*Ep. Men.* 127). You may be able to continue existing without clothing or shelter, but it will be cold and miserable. And absent food and hydration, you will soon die. Fortunately for us, these natural and necessary desires are easy to fulfil. Simply getting some rice and beans to fill your belly is not that big a deal. This is especially true if you are part of a network of friends willing to help each another out, in case anybody falls on hard times and has trouble even getting the basics needed to live comfortably. Furthermore, these desires are naturally limited. As Epicurus puts it, it is false to think that the stomach is insatiable and requires unlimited filling (*SV* 59). Instead, once you eat enough, you are full. Of course, eventually you will need more, but that is all right. It is still not true that, no matter how much you eat, you still need more. These desires you should try to fulfil, and you should try to plan out your life so that you can be confident that they will be fulfilled.

The vain and empty desires are the opposite of the natural and necessary ones in every way. Examples include desires for fame, power and wealth. Unlike natural and necessary desires, I do not have these instinctively. Instead, I learn them, usually from a sick society. Epicurus would be disgusted by the advertising industry and consumer culture, which he would regard as corrupting. These vain and empty desires are based on false opinions about what I need. For example, I might believe that having a sleek sports car will make me happy and bring me the respect and admiration of other people, as they stare at me, jaws agape, while I speed by in a stylish outfit and wraparound sunglasses. Sadly, if I were to get such a car, I would simply look like a pitiful academic undergoing a mid-life crisis, and soon I would grow bored with my toy, while still owing large monthly payments on it. It would be easy to multiply examples: Botox treatments, unnecessarily large houses, game consoles and so on.

Unlike natural and necessary desires, vain and empty desires have no natural limit. Indeed, they tend to increase without limit, and are thus very difficult to satisfy. No matter how much money I earn, I can always earn more. And I may think that I will be satisfied once I start making an annual salary of £50,000, but once I get there, it does not seem like so much, especially now that I know so many people who make even more. Similar considerations apply to fame and political power. And because they are unlimited, pursuing such desires tends to bring us into conflict with other people, especially when the form of the desire is not merely that I get lots and lots of X, but that I get more of X than those around me. These desires should be eliminated. Fortunately, because they are based on false opinions, uncovering these false opinions will help me get rid of them, once I realize that I do not need these things as I thought I did and that I would be happier without the desire for them.

The natural but not necessary desires are a little hazier. A scholion on *Principal Doctrine* 29 reports that they merely vary pleasure but do not remove pain, such as the desire for expensive foods. A report on the Epicurean attitude towards eating meat expands the idea slightly: meat is not needed to maintain our life, as we can do without it. In fact, eating meat is not conducive to health. Instead, it contributes just a "variation of pleasure", as do sex and drinking exotic wines.[3] The basic idea seems to be that it is natural to desire to eat when hungry, but not necessary (as far as assuaging one's hunger and restoring one's body to a healthy state) to eat a particular type of food. So a desire for a particular sort of luxurious food when hungry is natural but not necessary. The pleasure you get from eating filet mignon is different (although no greater) than the pleasure you get from eating rice and beans – hence these desires "vary" pleasure – but having this particular type of food is not needed to get rid of your hunger, so they do not remove pain. These sorts of desires should also be eliminated. They require intense effort to be fulfilled and, like the vain and empty desires, are based on groundless opinions (*KD* 30). Epicurus claims that people who are used to living simply and do not need extravagances are best equipped to enjoy extravagances when they happen to come along occasionally (*Ep. Men.* 130–31). The Epicureans do not think that we should *always* eschew luxury; if luxury happens to come along and can be obtained in a way that does not involve struggle or conflict with others, go ahead and indulge. But we must always be on guard not to develop desires that can be fulfilled only by such luxurious goods.

So Epicurus advocates eliminating all but the natural and necessary desires and living a fairly simple life as the best strategy for attaining pleasure. The greatest benefit of living like this is that it makes one self-sufficient. With few desires, you will suffer far less often from the pain of not having them satisfied, and one can easily gain the bodily pleasure of *aponia*. But far more importantly, you will have good grounds for confidence that the future will go well for you, as your desires are easily satisfied. So you will not suffer from the fear and anxiety that afflict those whose fortunes are dependent on the whims of chance. Hence, with this serene confidence, you will attain the mental pleasure of *ataraxia*.

It may be objected that the Epicurean life would be extremely boring. As we shall see, it includes a place for interacting with one's friends, studying philosophy and even worshipping the gods. Nonetheless, it may seem awfully limited: having just the basic desires, living simply and fulfilling them, and facing the future serenely. Would it not get stale? Epicurus would probably reply that such a life *would* be boring to many people, but that is because they are corrupt. As he puts it, ingratitude is what causes the greedy desire for unlimited variations in lifestyle (*SV* 69). A person who genuinely has reduced his desires as he should would be getting everything he desires by living simply, and he would be content.

THIRTEEN

The virtues and philosophy

Epicurus holds that only one's own pleasure has intrinsic value. A consequence of this is that anything else that has value must have value as either (i) a constituent of one's own pleasure or (ii) a means to one's own pleasure. Epicurus is rigorous in following out this implication of his basic ethical position.

Epicurus is happy to challenge many aspects of popular Greek morality on the basis of his moderately ascetic hedonism. For example, a person who endures great hardship and makes substantial sacrifices in his successful pursuit of political office would be regarded by Epicurus not as an admirable patriot but as a fool who is causing himself unnecessary trouble on the basis of a groundless opinion. And the touchy heroes of Homer who are willing to wreak great havoc in order to avenge slights are displaying not a high-minded concern for honour but destructive childishness, and they would do well to heed the adage "Sticks and stones may break my bones, but words can never hurt me".

Still, Epicurus wishes to institute a substantial modification of and reform to traditional Greek ethical ideals, not to repudiate them wholesale. Epicurus is no Callicles, the unbridled sensualist hedonist of Plato's dialogue the *Gorgias*, who regards conventional notions of justice and self-control as impediments to attaining pleasure, impediments the strong man rejects. Epicurus wishes to find places within his ethics for virtues such as moderation and courage, for philosophy and wisdom, for justice and friendship, and for reverence of the gods. In each case, he argues they are needed in order to live an untroubled life. In this chapter, we shall look at how he to tries accommodate the virtues and philosophy within his ethics.

The virtues

Epicurus says that prudence is the source of all of the other virtues, and that it is impossible to live pleasantly without having the virtues and living virtuously (*Ep. Men.* 132; *KD* 5). Virtues are valued solely because of their contribution towards living pleasantly, not for their own sake. Critics of Epicureanism such as Cicero raise the following two sets of hostile questions:

1. Is Epicurus right that you need to be virtuous in order to live pleasantly? Wouldn't clear-eyed pursuit of pleasure occasionally give one good reason to act viciously?
2. Is it acceptable to view the virtues as merely instrumental goods? Doesn't making the virtues handmaidens of pleasure debase the virtues? Is the person who regards the virtues in this way truly virtuous?

Let us turn to the case of moderation. Here, Epicurus seems to be on secure ground. The limit of pleasure is freedom from bodily pain and mental turmoil, and we should reduce our desires to the natural and necessary ones in order to live pleasantly. If you indulge yourself in gratifying natural but unnecessary desires for expensive wines, luxury foods or huge feasts by drinking heavily and gorging yourself, you hurt your bodily health, whereas living simply improves your bodily health. More importantly, such desires cause needless mental turmoil, as they are difficult to satisfy, whereas moderate people avoid these troubles.

Still, Epicurus makes it clear that he disdains such extravagant pleasures, not because they are bad *per se*, but because of the troubles they cause (Stob. *Anthology* 3.17.33, IG I-59). And this seems reasonable enough. As Epicurus puts it, we criticize profligate people because their way of life leads to distress. If drinking barrels of beer and eating large quantities of steak dissolved your fears about the gods and taught you to limit your desires, then the profligate would be filled with pleasure admixed with no pain, and that would be all right (*KD* 10). But, as a matter of fact, that is not what happens to them.

Courage would initially seem a harder case for the Epicureans. After all, the two constituents of the highest good are freedom from bodily pain and freedom from mental distress, which is supposed to be primarily based on the confidence that you will not be in bodily pain. And, it might be argued, this should justify many behaviours that would conventionally be considered cowardly, in order to avoid bodily pain and the anticipation of it.

Although the Epicureans would reject some acts conventionally deemed courageous as actually foolhardy, they basically stick to their guns and insist that the wise person will be courageous. First of all, they note that the main motivator of cowardly behaviour is the fear of death, and the wise person realizes that there is nothing to fear in death (Cic. *Fin.* I 49). They also maintain – optimistically and mistakenly – that truly severe pains do not last long, as severe enough pains are followed shortly by death. (Sufferers from congestive heart failure, rheumatoid arthritis combined with advanced osteoporosis, severe but non-lethal burns over much of one's body, and many other conditions could rightly call out the Epicureans on this point.)

The Epicurean defence of courage follows the same general pattern as their defences of justice and friendship (which we examine in the next two chapters). Fools focus too much on short-term consequences, and they are willing to break the social compact and betray others for the sake of short-term advantage, without realizing the terrible impact behaving in this way has on one's peace of mind. In Cicero's *On Ends*, the spokesman for the Epicurean position, Torquatus, tries to show how the illustrious deeds of his ancestor in battle could be justified on hedonistic grounds. His deeds were painful and dangerous in the short term, but they helped to provide for the safety of his fellow citizens and hence for himself. Also, he did his deeds in view of others and thus gained their esteem. This sort of reputation leads others to trust you and help you in turn (Cic. *Fin.* I 35).

Most Greek philosophers – Plato, Aristotle and the Stoics, at a minimum – would find this account of the value of courage and the motives of the courageous man repugnant. Aristotle, for instance, believes that the virtues are perfections of our nature as human beings – as rational and social animals – and that when we live virtuously we are living well as human beings. Virtuous actions are intrinsically valuable, not valuable merely for their consequences, and such actions are the main constituent of a happy and flourishing human life. Moreover, the truly virtuous person recognizes that such actions are admirable expressions of human perfection, and he does them for this very reason. As Aristotle puts it, he does them for the sake of *to kalon*, the noble or the fine (*Eth. Nic.* III 1116a11, and elsewhere).[1] A person who behaves courageously, but does so only for the sake of the good consequences and not because the action itself is noble and fine, is not truly courageous, but pseudo-courageous (*Eth. Nic.* III viii). Epicurus yields no ground before such high-minded criticisms, however, saying that he spits on the noble and on those who vainly admire it, whenever it does not produce pleasure (Ath. *Deipnosophists* 12, 547a [IG I-151]).

Still, while Epicurus considers the virtues to be merely handmaidens of pleasure, he thinks that being virtuous is both necessary *and sufficient* for living a pleasant life: that is, not only must you be virtuous to live pleasantly, but being virtuous guarantees that you will live pleasantly (*Ep. Men.* 132; *KD* 5). So, Epicurus maintains that the wise person will be happy even on the rack (*DL* X 188), a thesis Aristotle regards as absurd (*Eth. Nic.* I 1095b32–1096a2). And it is difficult to see any justification within Epicureanism for it; on a view like the Stoics', in which happiness and virtue are identified, there is at least a rationale for viewing the tortured wise man as happy, although Aristotle would regard it as a *reductio* and not merely a consequence of the view. Within Epicureanism, it looks like a piece of bluster. Still, in putting forward this view, Epicurus joins ranks with many who think that a person's happiness cannot be lost by merely contingent events, and he himself writes in his final day that he is exceedingly happy despite his physical agony caused by urinary blockages (*Ep. Id.*, *DL* X 22, IG I-41).

Philosophy

Wisdom itself is given the same sort of justification as the other virtues. Practically speaking, wisdom is needed to engage in the sort of cost–benefit analysis of desires discussed in Chapter 12: we need to use our reason in order to realize that the natural and necessary desires are limited and easy to fulfil, and should be fulfilled, whereas the other sorts of desires are based on groundless opinions and should be rejected. Infants are ruled by the pleasure principle, going for whatever pleasure immediately beckons. As adults we are still at root motivated by the desire for pleasure. But we need to move from the pleasure principle to the reality principle, delaying gratification when needed. Virtues such as courage come to be through a calculation of what is advantageous (*DL* X 120), and this is why Epicurus says practical wisdom (*phronesis*, also translated as "prudence") is the source of all of the other virtues.

In order to attain happiness, however, such practical wisdom regarding the consequences of our actions and the limits of our desires is not enough. We also need "theoretical" wisdom: a proper understanding of the principles of atomism and how they can explain the world around us. As Epicurus puts it, even if we gain security from other people, this will not be enough to help us live securely if we are still troubled about the possibility of harm from the gods or the other creatures depicted in superstitious myths. And if you are ignorant about the nature of the universe, you cannot get rid of these fears. You need natural science to understand the true causes of natural phenomena and dispel such fears (*KD* 11–13).

The other fear that theoretical wisdom helps dispel is the fear of death. As we shall see, Epicurus argues that there is nothing to fear in death, *if* death is annihilation. But a proper understanding of the corporeal nature of the mind – that it is a bodily organ, perishing along with the rest of the body on death – is needed to grasp that death *is* annihilation. Without such an understanding, fear of the unknown in death would still plague us.

As with courage, this explanation of the value of wisdom would strike somebody like Aristotle as debased. For Aristotle, the highest part of humanity is reason. And the activity of understanding God and the cosmos is the highest expression of our reason, and as such is valuable for its own sake, not just because it secures us peace of mind. Indeed, if the Epicureans stick to their thesis that all mental pleasures are ultimately based on bodily pleasures (through memory or anticipation), they cannot even say that we find understanding the cosmos or other intellectual activities pleasurable in themselves. (Plutarch clucks disapprovingly in *A Pleasant Life* 1093c that the Epicureans reject even the pleasures of mathematics.) As noted earlier, Lucretius seems to admit that learning the hidden workings of nature fills him with an awestruck pleasure. And Epicurus says that the process of learning philosophy is pleasant (*SV* 27) and that the wise person takes more pleasure in contemplation than do others (*DL* X 120). But in both cases, the explanation of the pleasure would probably be in terms of the way in which learning helps drive out anxiety.

The Epicureans hold that philosophizing produces mental health (*SV* 54), just as medicine produces bodily health. This trope is common, going back at least to Plato (e.g. *Grg.* 521e–522a). But the Epicureans take the analogy very strictly: nobody thinks that surgery or cough syrup are good *per se*, apart from their promotion of bodily health, so too with argumentation and psychic health – "Empty is the argument of the philosopher which heals no human disease; for just as there is no benefit in medicine if it does not drive out bodily diseases, so there is no benefit in philosophy if it does drive out the disease of the mind".[2]

Quotations like this may raise the suspicion that Epicurus is urging us to believe the Epicurean theses about atoms, the gods and the mind simply because they are comforting, and that he seeks to revive the Democritean atomist worldview because of its effectiveness in combating fears of the gods and death. But this is not quite right. After all, the following inference is invalid:

1. Believing p would be comforting to me.
2. Therefore, p.

Such wishful thinking cannot provide a secure foundation for psychic health. Epicurus thinks that only the wise person is unshakeably persuaded of anything, and a repeated refrain of Lucretius is that we must study the underlying principles of nature in order to dispel the terrifying darkness that covers our minds.[3] So the Epicurean arguments in physics are supposed to establish, in the usual way, that their conclusions are true, not merely that believing them helps us feel good. The pragmatic justification comes in, instead, to answer the question of why we should bother to engage in the activity of trying to understand the workings of the world in the first place. And here, the Epicureans appeal not to the intrinsic value of understanding the world or how this activity is the fulfilment of human nature, but to how it secures tranquillity: ignorance is not bliss.

Still, with their stress on practical effectiveness above all else, it seems like the Epicureans would have no bar in theory in putting forward bad but effective arguments, or in using techniques that are (from a rational point of view) dubious. And some of the actual Epicurean techniques might seem to bear this out.[4]

The Epicureans are convinced that Epicurus is not merely the discoverer of many interesting and cogent arguments. Instead, he is the saviour of humanity, and the only route to salvation from superstitious fears and empty desires is by fully accepting his message. Because of this, even though Epicurus' arguments *are* supposed to be cogent, the Epicureans are interested in producing fervent disciples, not dispassionate critical thinkers. The Epicureans encourage a fawning adulation of Epicurus, as expressed in Lucretius' glowing descriptions of Epicurus as our redeemer (*DRN* I 62–79) and as a god (*DRN* V 8). Naturally, this goes along with viewing Epicurus as an authority figure whose wisdom we need to accept. In the eulogy to Epicurus that opens the third book of *De Rerum Natura*, Lucretius declaims "You are our father and the discoverer of truth: you supply us with fatherly precepts; and from your pages, illustrious master, like the bees which in flowerful vales sip each bloom, we sip on each golden saying – golden and ever most worthy of eternal life" (*DRN* III 9–13; trans. in Smith 2001).

The flipside of this attitude is that other philosophical positions are regarded as not merely mistaken but pernicious. Epicurean texts are filled with invective and abuse towards other philosophers. The Epicureans are far from unique in this regard, but they do stand out as particularly vitriolic.[5] The goal of Epicurean pedagogy is not to give a full, fair and sympathetic hearing toward other philosophers, but to equip students with the arguments and attitudes they need in order to reject destructive falsehood and embrace healing truth. The contrast with thinkers such as Aristotle and Cicero is instructive. Cicero, for example, often expresses his own contempt for Epicureanism. Still, as a self-professed Academic and follower of Socrates, Cicero believes he must give the case for the philosophical positions of Epicureans and others as best he can, setting up the arguments *pro* and *contra*, so that his readers can come to their own good-faith evaluations of which position is the most plausible. Such open-minded exploration of the arguments is constitutive of the philosophical enterprise.[6]

Epicurus thinks that all people, young and old, need correct philosophy to produce psychic health and happiness (*Ep. Men.* 122), and Epicurus was notably egalitarian in admitting women and slaves to his school. But not all people are ready or able to follow the detailed arguments that establish the truth of Epicureanism, so correct philosophy must be delivered to them by other means. At the start of the *Letter to Herodotus*, Epicurus states that he wrote the summary of the main points of his physics for people who are unable to work through the details of his arguments for these conclusions, and he encourages firm memorization of the most general doctrines. A similar goal is served by producing a list of the *Principal Doctrines*: short statements of the main points to remember.

The Epicureans are probably correct that techniques such as reverence of a saviour figure, scorn of outsiders and memorization of key doctrines are effective means for promoting orthodoxy. But they provoked the scorn of high-minded critics such as Arcesilaus, who turned the Academy in a sceptical direction shortly after Epicurus' death. When asked why other philosophical schools regularly lost followers to the Epicureans, whereas Epicureans never went over to other schools, he cracked that men can become eunuchs, but eunuchs can never become men (*DL* IV 43).

FOURTEEN

Justice

Epicurus develops an innovative social contract theory of justice. Justice is a human invention, which comes into existence when we gather together to form communities and agree not to harm one another. Apart from such an agreement, there is no justice. The particulars of what is just depend on the content of the agreement that we make with one another, and justice is thus relative from place to place and time to time. This, however, does not make justice "merely" conventional or relative in a way that undermines its authority or gives the wise person any reason to be unjust. Epicurus strives to repair problems afflicting earlier versions of a social contract theory, such as that advanced by Glaucon in book two of Plato's *Republic*. Still, despite his defence of justice, Epicurus advocates a life that avoids political engagement.

Epicurean contractarianism and its implications

The "justice of nature" is an agreement not to harm one another, which is useful for the parties to the agreement (*KD* 31). Human beings form societies in order to escape the dangers of living in a pre-social state of nature, such as starvation, death from exposure to the elements and animal attacks (*DRN* V 982–1028). Agreeing to cooperate with one another in order to protect ourselves from such dangers is beneficial to everybody. But in order to have a functioning society, in which the members are able to live free of fear, we need to have agreements about how to treat one another. For instance, worrying about somebody hitting me with a baseball bat in order to take my food as I exit a shop would get in the way of my happiness, as would actually being hit on the head with the bat, and so we prohibit assault.

Where there is such an agreement about how to behave, actions can be just or unjust, according to whether they conform to or violate the agreement. When I drive on the right-hand side of the road in Atlanta, I am behaving justly, whereas the person who viciously tries to hit me in order to grab my bananas is behaving unjustly. Apart from such an actually obtaining social agreement, however, there is no justice. In a clear swipe at thinkers such as Plato, Epicurus denies that justice exists *per se*; instead, its existence is parasitic on the existence of agreements (*KD* 33).

Epicurus is not shy about drawing out the implications of this theory (*KD* 32). There is no justice (or injustice) with respect to animals that cannot make an agreement about not harming one another. So if we pack tens of thousands of chickens together in horrible surroundings, pump them full of antibiotics in order to prevent disease and then debeak them so that they will be less likely to mutilate one another despite being driven mad by their living conditions, we are not doing anything unjust to the chickens. (If the concept of natural rights were explained to him, Epicurus would probably agree with Bentham that it is nonsense on stilts.) And if a pride of lions was preying on our village, it would be nice if we could talk to the lions and say to them, "Please don't hurt us, and we will not hurt you. Why not confine your hunting to the gazelles instead?" But as the lions cannot reply to our entreaties and agree to refrain from preying on us, we will simply wipe them out instead to protect ourselves, and there is nothing unjust in doing so (Porph. *Abst.* I.12.5–6, LS 22N).[1] Likewise, if one nation invades and conquers another simply for the sake of national glory, and there is no non-aggression treaty or framework of international law that the invasion violates, then the invasion is not unjust (or just).

Still, we need to be careful not to overstate these implications. "Just" and "unjust" do not exhaust the universe of ethical appraisal; actions can be *foolish* or *vicious* without being *unjust*. So, for example, while the lion slaughter would be condoned by Epicureans, the factory-farming of the chickens would be condemned, not because it violates chicken-rights, but because of the environmental degradation caused by the practice and the harmful effects of eating meat on one's health (Porph. *Abst.* I.44.2–I.55.4). And aggressive wars spurred by a desire for glory are a stupid negative-sum practice, spreading destruction and suffering for everyone involved for no good reason. Even if they are not unjust, they should be avoided, and enlightened legislators should seek to institute a framework of treaties and international law in order to render such wars unjust and lessen their likelihood.

Another implication of Epicurean contractarianism that Epicurus does not shy away from is that it entails a form of relativism. The exact form the social contract takes can vary from place to place, so the same things need not be just for everyone (*KD* 36). Let us imagine a small island society that is heavily dependant on fishing for its food. This society may ban catching and keeping fish below a certain length, to ensure that the stocks not be depleted. Catching and keeping a nine-inch-long haddock would be unjust for a member of that society, whereas it would be just for a person fishing in a society without such a prohibition.

Still, this form of relativism is fairly modest. It does not imply that the standards of justice are entirely determined by the laws of a society, or by the opinions of that society's members about what is just. There is an objective standard we can use to evaluate the laws and agreements of a society: whether they are useful. The basic conception of justice is that justice is what is useful for the needs of living with one another (*KD* 37). Laws that do not meet this standard are not just laws. For example, laws against assault will almost certainly be useful, but anti-miscegenation laws (laws banning interracial sex and/or marriage) would not be. So, generally speaking, what will be just is the same, in so far as what is useful for people living together – such as prohibiting assault – is the same. But this allows for a fair amount of variation from place to place and time to time, including laws that were just at one point no longer being just after they become outmoded (*KD* 37–8).

This objective standard for evaluating the justice of laws and agreements is not inconsistent with Epicurus' metaphysics or his contractarianism. Justice does not exist *per se*. Instead, we bring it into existence through our agreements about how to behave when we form societies. Thus, we can rightly view justice as a sort of artefact. However, this does not make justice "artificial", in the sense of being arbitrary or unnatural. Epicurus strikingly asserts that the justice *of nature* is an agreement; that is, justice is both a human invention and natural. That is because human beings are rational beings, and so they naturally make such agreements for the sake of living together peaceably and securing their mutual advantage. Since the agreements we make are supposed to serve a purpose (as with other artefacts), we have a standard whereby to evaluate the agreements: whether they successfully fulfil their purpose.

Free riders and the Ring of Gyges

Even if we admit that justice is generally useful, this still leaves open the question of why *I* should be just. In book two of Plato's *Republic*, Glaucon and Adeimantus describe a social contract theory of justice that resembles Epicurus' in many respects. But because on this theory justice is good only because of its consequences, they conclude that there will be times when the rationally self-interested person would do what is unjust. Epicurus wishes to avoid this conclusion.

Before moving on to the *Republic*, however, it will be useful to first discuss the "free rider problem". Let us imagine a case in which a collective action is to the benefit of each of the individual members of the group. For instance, I may be one of a group of shepherds. We have a common meadow for our sheep to graze in. If we allow our sheep to graze for hours and hours each day, the meadow will become overgrazed, which will hurt our flocks. On the other hand, allowing each of our flocks to graze for one hour every day would be enough to feed our sheep while having the meadow flourish and sustain our flocks in the long run. So as a rationally self-interested shepherd, it seems, I would endorse the cooperative scheme of limiting our grazing times, as I would be better off under it than I would be under the unlimited grazing regime.

But this leads directly to the free rider problem. Suppose that I have the opportunity to sneak my sheep on to the meadow at night and fatten them up, outside my scheduled time. Then, it seems, I should take advantage of the opportunity and violate the agreement, thereby becoming a "free rider". After all, as long as everybody else adheres to the agreement, I still get the benefit of the meadow remaining healthy – my own small violation will not be enough on its own to ruin the meadow – while also getting the benefit of the extra time and the fatter, healthier sheep. But if every rationally self-interested shepherd engages in the same sort of calculation, then the cooperative scheme soon collapses. The individual pursuit of self-interest leads collectively to a sub-optimal result.

Two sorts of common responses to this problem would not be available to Epicurus. The first is that, having given my consent to the agreement, it would be morally wrong for me to cheat. But Epicurus says that injustice is not bad *per se*, but bad only because of its consequences, and the idea of a moral constraint on one's behaviour divorced from considerations of self-interest would be profoundly foreign to the whole Epicurean way of thinking about what one should do. The second, Kantian, response is that it would be inconsistent and irrational for me to expect all of the other members of my group to adhere to an agreement while exempting myself from that requirement. But even though Epicurus emphasizes that the wise person recognizes the general usefulness of justice and that this recognition gives him a reason to be just, Epicurean ethics is fundamentally a matter of *me* deciding what to do based on what is in *my* interest. My decision might be different if I were legislating for all people and were required to apply to myself the same standards I apply to others, but that is not the situation that I find myself in, unfortunately.

To prevent free-riding and preserve the benefits of cooperation, what we need is an enforcement mechanism: punishment for those who defect from the agreement. So we do not simply voluntarily agree to limit our grazing time and set a schedule. Instead, we hire a group of guards to watch over the meadow, who are charged to use their truncheons to beat anybody who tries to sneak on to the meadow outside his scheduled time and to leave him there as a warning to others. As a rationally self-interested individual, I agree to this enforcement mechanism, in order to keep people like me from cheating.

But if my only reason for adhering to the agreement is that I will be punished if I am caught breaking the agreement, then it seems I would break the agreement when I am certain of getting away with the violation. This is precisely the conclusion that Glaucon draws in his famous story of the Ring of Gyges, a ring that allows its wearer to become invisible at will. Glaucon describes a nasty state of nature, which individuals escape by forming a society and agreeing not to hurt one another. This agreement is the origin of justice, and society institutes punishments to enforce justice. But any person with the ring would act unjustly and would be right to do so: he would kill the king, seize his throne, sleep with his wife and enrich himself.

Epicurus has a two-pronged response to try to avoid this unsavoury conclusion. First, he agrees with Glaucon that injustice is not bad *per se*, but only because of punishment and the fear of punishment (*KD* 34). The *fear* of punishment, however, plays a huge role here. Even if you "get away" with your injustice, you can never be certain that at some point in the future you will not get caught, so you still suffer bad consequences from committing injustice (*KD* 35). And because tranquillity is the main constituent of the happy life for Epicurus, having to live in fear of punishment is reason enough never to break the law: it is not worth it. Glaucon might insist that it is part of his thought experiment that you can be 100 per cent sure that you will never be caught, so that Epicurus' reply is beside the point. But Epicurus is profoundly hostile to doing ethics via this sort of thought experiment. He is the sort of annoying fellow who would reply that even if you found the Ring of Gyges, you would still have to worry that perhaps it has been planted by a nefarious government agency with a microchip embedded in it, or that it is powered by a tiny battery that could give out just as you are sneaking into the king's bedchambers.

Secondly, and more importantly, Epicurus disagrees with Glaucon on the benefits of injustice. For Glaucon, neither suffering nor committing injustice is a second best. It is better than both suffering and committing injustice, but not as good as being able to commit injustice while not suffering it (*Rep.* 358e–359b). But Epicurus says that the laws exist for the sake of the wise, not so that they will not commit injustice, but so that they will not suffer it (Stob. *Anthology* 4.143, IG I-154). The wise Epicurean knows he has no need for wealth or luxury goods, and he is not troubled by resentment or hatred. So he would have no motive to harm others in any case (*DL* X 117). The fear of punishment is needed only to keep fools in line. A community of wise Epicureans would be full of justice, but it would have no need of laws and punishments.[2]

The wise Epicurean has the virtue of justice: a disposition to behave justly (that is, to adhere to the agreement neither to harm nor be harmed) and to do so for the right reason (that is, because he recognizes the general usefulness of the agreement for promoting the *ataraxia* of his community and of himself, and because he has no temptation to break the agreement anyway, and not merely because of the fear of punishment). As with the other virtues, one cannot live pleasantly without living justly (*Ep. Men.* 132; *KD* 5).

Epicureans and the political life

Although the wise Epicurean will be just, he will avoid getting involved in the business of politics (*DL* X 119; *SV* 58). The justification for this is straightforward: engagement with the hurly-burly of politics is risky and a bad strategy for achieving tranquillity. Epicurus writes that the "natural good" of things such as political office, power and fame is security from other people (*KD* 6–7). But even though power and wealth provide some security from others, a quiet life and withdrawal from the many are much more effective means (*KD* 14; *DRN* V 1117–35).[3]

So it may seem that the Epicurean is, after all, a sort of free-rider. While it is necessary to have people engage in civic life, to craft laws well for the sake of ensuring the smooth functioning of society, the wise Epicurean is content to leave that hard and troublesome work to others while reaping the rewards. Epicurean principles would provide good grounds for criticizing existing laws as not being just, because they are not useful. But it is far from clear that an Epicurean would work to overturn such laws rather than simply trying to hide away in order not to be disturbed by them. Furthermore, the same grounds that the wise Epicurean has for not acting unjustly – punishment and the fear of punishment – would also give him reason not to break laws that are not just. For instance, the Epicurean Metrodorus counsels against engaging in sex in ways that breaks the law or disturbs conventions (*SV* 51). Now, Metrodorus does speak of the conventions being "proper and well-established" ones, but the wise Epicurean living in Virginia in the 1950s, it seems, would be better off simply going along with anti-miscegenation laws, as he has little to gain and much to lose by breaking them, even though they are not just.

The Epicureans do not withdraw entirely from society, however. Instead, the Garden and other Epicurean communities operate as best they can as part of the larger non-Epicurean society. Within the Epicurean communities, the members strive to perfectly embody the principles of Epicureanism, especially its views on justice. By providing a model of rational and tranquil community life, and by engaging in the activity of proselytizing others to join this community, Epicureans can serve as a catalyst for social reform even without engaging directly in the irksome business of politics.

FIFTEEN

Friendship

Epicurus praises friendship in extravagant terms, calling it an "immortal good" (*SV* 78), which "dances round the world announcing to us all that we should wake to blessedness" (*SV* 52). This is because friendship is by far the greatest thing for making our whole life blessed (*KD* 27). Knowing that we can count on our friends to help us out in times of need allows us to face the future fearlessly. But in order to have such friends, we must in turn help our friends out when they need us. So the Epicureans believe they can accommodate friendship within their egoistic hedonism. In fact, they even claim that there is good prudential reason to love your friend as much as yourself. Egoistically loving your friend as much as yourself is a difficult trick to pull off, and it may seem that in the case of friendship, at least, Epicurus abandons his strict psychological egoism. This is probably not true. However, some later Epicureans did advance such non-egoistic theories, and while they are inconsistent with key tenets of Epicureanism, they are also, arguably, closer to the psychological phenomena of friendship.

The security of friendship

Just as courage comes to be by reasoning out what is advantageous, so too does friendship come to be because of its usefulness (*DL*

X 120). The main reason given by Epicureans for the importance of friendship is that it provides safety: with friends to protect you, your life will be secure from danger, whereas the friendless life is beset with risks (Cic. *Fin.* I 65–66). Even a person who has limited his desires as he should would have to worry about being unable to fulfil them if he has to go it alone. Epicurus says that the wise person wishes to have friends so that he might have somebody to attend him when he is sick and help him when he is imprisoned or impoverished (Sen. *Ep.* 9.8, IG I-54).

Friends provide a kind of "mutual aid" society; the friends protect one another from danger and provide for one another in time of need. If you are surrounded by friends, and thus able to eliminate all fear of your neighbours, your life will be most pleasant (*KD* 40). Epicurean friendship is communal. Its focus is not on the one-on-one interaction between friends, but on how having a network of friends who look out for one another is beneficial to all. In their communities, Epicureans tried to implement this type of friendship.[1]

Having friends, therefore, will help you avoid both bodily pain and mental distress. When your friends help you out in times of sickness or hunger, this improves your bodily state and helps you achieve *aponia*, the limit of bodily pleasure. But having reason not to fear that you *will be* in great bodily pain, and thus achieving *ataraxia*, is far more important to happiness. It is for this reason that Epicurus maintains that it is not so much the actual help from our friends that we need, but confidence that they *will* help us (*SV* 34).

A network of friends can also provide an *intellectual* mutual aid society. Friendship among Epicureans reinforces proper philosophy, provides models of conduct and helps prevent vain desires from developing. Forthright philosophical discussion and censure are central to Epicurean pedagogy, and this practice of speaking frankly is considered part of "the office of a friend".[2] Epicurus recommends practising his ethical precepts with like-minded friends in order to avoid disturbance (*Ep. Men.* 135). Within an Epicurean community, being surrounded by right-thinking compatriots helps to sustain one on the straight and narrow. There were even mugs featuring portraits of Epicurus, celebrations of his birthday and the like, to help bring the community members together and reinforce Epicurus' teachings.[3]

Egoistically loving your friend as much as yourself

So the Epicureans have excellent reason to value friendship and to praise it in high-flown terms. Nonetheless, regarding your friends as a kind of "mutual aid society" may seem inadequate for true friendship. At the end of Cicero's exposition of Epicurean ethics in book one of *On Ends*, the Epicurean spokesman Torquatus defends Epicureanism against the charge that hedonism would make true friendship impossible, and he insists that Epicureanism can accommodate even the demand that a true friend will love his friend as much as himself. Torquatus admits there is a variety of ways Epicureans try to accommodate this demand, and he presents three different Epicurean theories of friendship.

Proponents of the first theory start from the unimpeachably Epicurean observation that, like the virtues, friendship is only instrumentally valuable and deserves to be cultivated only because it allows us to live securely (Cic. *Fin.* I 68, II 82). And they admit that we do not value our friends' pleasures and pains in themselves as we do our own (Cic. *Fin.* I 66). Still, the wise person recognizes that he needs friendship to attain the greatest pleasure for himself. Furthermore, he recognizes that friendship requires us to love our friends as much as ourselves. And so, on egoistic grounds, he does love his friends as much as he does himself: he feels exactly the same towards his friend as towards himself and exerts himself as much for his friend's pleasure as for his own (Cic. *Fin.* I 66–8).

At least initially, this theory suffers from two obvious problems. The first involves the final ends of the Epicurean sage, who supposedly loves his friend as much as himself because loving him in this way is the most effective means for securing his own pleasure. Either (i) the theory is inconsistent in how it describes the final ends of the Epicurean sage, asserting that the sage values only his own pleasure for its own sake and also that he values his friends and his friends' pleasures as much as his own. Or, consistently within itself, (ii) the theory ascribes an inconsistent set of motives to the wise person, making him suffer from a serious case of doublethink: the sage values his friends' pleasures as much as his own, while recognizing that he does so for the sake of his own pleasure, the only thing he regards as valuable in itself.

Secondly, the process of coming to love your friend as much as yourself seems to suffer from psychological implausibility: is it possible to decide, on egoistic grounds, to cultivate a disinterested love of others? As Cicero points out (*Fin.* II 78), genuine affection does not usually result from calculations of expediency. Now, people *can* play all sorts of mind games with themselves. For instance, consider the person described in Pascal's wager (*Pensées* §233), who cannot believe in God initially, but gets himself sprinkled with holy water, has masses said for himself and engages in other sorts of trickery in order to make himself believe in God, because he thinks that having this belief is prudent. But even if a person could cultivate religious belief by following Pascal's recommendation – and I believe he could – this sort of process, applied to friendship, would not be endorsed by the Epicureans, who prize prudent, clear-eyed rationality above all else.

Given these problems, one might be tempted to conclude that the Epicureans' position on friendship is inconsistent with their overall psychology and ethics, and this conclusion has often been drawn.[4] But these problems stem from assuming that the wise Epicurean loves his friends as much as himself in the sense that he *values* his friends' pleasures as much as he values his own. The problems dissolve, however, if we interpret the talk about "loving one's friend as much as oneself" in *behavioural* terms, that is, as prescribing a policy of action, instead of describing what one ultimately values. We desire pleasure for ourselves, and we see that friendship is one of the best means of attaining that end. If we are wise, however, we will also realize that we must *treat* our friends as well as we *treat* ourselves in order to have a stable friendship. Only by acting in this way can we build up the mutual trust that is the foundation of friendship. Thus, on egoistic grounds, we do treat our friends as well as we treat ourselves, and in this sense we love them as we do ourselves.[5]

Fools do not see this, so they are willing to betray their friends when not betraying them would involve significant pain and sacrifice. But the wise person realizes that failing to come through for his friends would destroy his reputation, so he is willing to go to great lengths to help his friend. In fact, the wise person will sometimes die for his friend (*DL* X 121). This may appear inconsistent with egoism, but remember that the Epicureans believe that death is "nothing to us". If you betray your friend, your life will be totally upset and confounded (*SV* 56–7), just as you would always live in fear that you *might* be caught if you break the laws, even if you were never caught (*KD* 34–5). So if you have to choose between dying for your friend and betraying your friend (and thus living out an anxious, upset life), the prudent thing to do would be to die for your friend.

The third Epicurean theory of friendship (Cic. *Fin.* I 70) is more forthright than the first in making love a matter of one's behaviour. (We shall look at the second theory shortly.) According to the third theory, wise people make an agreement between themselves to love each other as much as they love themselves, because doing so is conducive to living pleasantly. So this theory assimilates the Epicurean position on friendship to their position on justice. Justice is an agreement to neither harm nor be harmed, a pact of mutual non-interference, whereas friendship is an agreement to treat one another as well as one treats oneself, a pact of mutual beneficence.

A heterodox account of friendship

Just as in the case of justice, critics of Epicurean hedonism could argue that the clear-eyed pursuit of pleasure would sometimes justify immoral actions, such as breaking your word to your friend when you thereby stand to gain a great deal and can do so with impunity (see e.g. *Fin.* II 51–5). Still, given the Epicurean doctrine that peace of mind is the greatest pleasure, they have at least a plausible argument that the wise person will treat his friend as well as he treats himself. The more fundamental objection to the Epicureans is that, even if we grant that the wise person would care for his friend in this way, this sense of "loving" one's friend as much as oneself is too niggardly to deserve the name "love". The Epicurean "friend" may behave well, but given his motives and the way he regards his friend, he is still cold-hearted and selfish. And some later Epicureans are apparently impressed enough by this sort of objection that they are willing to make important modifications to Epicurean psychology to answer it. They offer the second theory of friendship recounted at the end of book one of *On Ends* (*Fin.* I 69).

These "timid" Epicureans (as Torquatus calls them) offer their alternative account because they fear that friendship would be totally crippled if we sought it only for the sake of our own pleasure. Their identity is unclear, but Cicero says that they are recent Epicureans and that their position is an innovation, never put forward by Epicurus himself (*Fin.* II 82). The first century BCE Epicurean Philodemus was probably one of them (see Tsouna 2007: 27–31). According to these Epicureans, our initial interactions with our friends are motivated entirely by a desire for our own pleasure, but later we can develop a love for our friends that is *not* rooted in a desire for our own pleasure, whereas in the first theory the desire for pleasure continues to be our sole motive later on. Spending time together engenders familiarity, so that we come to love our friends for their own sake, even if we gain no advantage from the friendship. This is likened to the process whereby we (supposedly) come to have disinterested affection for pets, familiar activities, our home city and the like, by repeated association with them. In the second theory, it is explicitly denied that friendship is desirable only for the sake of our own pleasure.

Once I have this sort of affection for my friends, it also opens up a different sort of hedonistic justification for friendship. With familiarity, I become fond of locales and pets. So I enjoy hanging out by the neighbourhood convenience store watching pierced teenagers asking passersby for cigarettes, even if being there serves no further purpose of mine like getting food. Likewise, petting my mangy old cat is soothing, even if she is totally worthless otherwise. My friends offer much richer opportunities for these sorts of pleasures. Spending time with them is enjoyable, and this pleasure need not be reduced to considerations of how they will have my back, unlike on the first theory. If we wish, we could try to fit this into the Epicurean framework of desires by positing a natural and necessary desire for friendship, in which having friends is necessary for happiness, although not for life itself, and where we desire friendship for its own sake, not simply for the sake of satisfying some further desire, such as for food or shelter.

Cicero, for one, says that this sort of theory is humane (*Fin.* II 82). But embracing it would require considerable deviation from orthodoxy. Most fundamentally, it gives up psychological hedonism and egoism, as with time we come to care about our friends for their own sake, apart from any usefulness derived from the relationship. That my motives in the beginning were self-seeking does not alter this point. And because Epicurean ethics is based on Epicurean psychology, these heterodox Epicureans are going to have difficulties in maintaining the fundamental tenet that only our own pleasure is valuable once they admit that we care about things other than our own pleasure.

Nor is this point altered by noting that pursuing friendship can be justified on hedonistic grounds. Let us presume that I care for my friend for his own sake, and that as a result I enjoy hanging out with him and helping him out. Then I would have excellent hedonistic reasons to spend time with my friend and to benefit him: doing so is pleasurable. As David Hume points out, though, the fact that I get pleasure from interacting with my friend does not show that I value my friend *for the sake of* the pleasure. If the explanation for my why I enjoy interacting with my friend is that I care about him for his own sake, then I care about him for his own sake.[6]

Let us leave aside this problem: perhaps a revisionist Epicurean could say that we simply find spending time with our friends enjoyable in itself, without rooting this enjoyment in a concern for our friends' welfare for their own sake, any more than I care about the welfare of the neighbourhood convenience store, even though I am fond of the place. This account of the pleasures of friendship is plausible, more plausible than the theory that the pleasures of friendship are based on expectations of security and memories of benefits. But it would require abandoning the thesis that all mental pleasures depend on bodily pleasures. It is not just by oversight that orthodox Epicureans describe the value of friendship in terms of the security from physical danger that it provides; instead, it follows from their view of the dependence of mental pleasures on bodily ones. As Cicero notes, Epicurus would never allow that pursuits such as literature and learning are pleasurable in themselves, and Torquatus agrees with this, although he also says that some later Epicureans do allow for some mental pleasures that do not arise out of bodily ones (*Fin.* I 25, 55).[7]

In short, orthodox Epicureans can make a very strong case for the importance of friendship and of treating your friends well. But the ways in which orthodox Epicureanism tries to explain the particulars of how we regard our friends and how we find friendship pleasurable is inadequate, and these inadequacies put serious pressure on Epicurean psychology.

SIXTEEN

The gods

A central goal of Epicurean physics is to banish the fear of the gods, because that fear is one of the chief impediments to attaining happiness. We have already looked (in Chapter 5) at the negative side of Epicurean theology. The workings of the cosmos can be explained entirely in terms of the purposeless motions, reboundings and entanglements of atoms moving through the void, and so there is no reason to attribute them to the gods (*DRN* V 1161–1225). Furthermore, the manifest flaws in the world show that it is not under the control of philanthropic deities, and the random ways in which phenomena such as lightning bolts occur show that they are not the result of *any* sort of agency, even the jealous and flawed agency of the Olympian gods.

Since the Epicureans eject the gods from the world, denying that they have any influence whatsoever on it, it is understandable that "Epicurean" became a byword for "atheist" in antiquity. (In fact, a Hebrew word for an unbelieving heretic, an *apikoros*, is derived from "Epicurean".) But the Epicureans vigorously rebut this accusation. Epicurus pointedly calls some of the prominent atheists of his time crazy, comparing them to people in a Bacchic frenzy (Phld. *Piet.* 112.5–12, LS 23H). He says that the knowledge that there are gods is *enargēs*, evident or obvious. *Enargēs* is the same term he uses to label obvious and evident phenomena such as there being bodies in motion, phenomena on the basis of which we make inferences about what is hidden, the *adēlon*. *Why* the existence of the gods is supposed to be so obvious is itself, unfortunately, unclear. In Cicero's *On the Nature of the Gods*, our main source for Epicurean theology, the Epicurean spokesman offers the inadequate but widespread argument from common consensus: all human beings have a naturally occurring, innate preconception of the gods and that they exist, and so they do (*Nat. D.* I 43–4).

Our basic grasp (*prolēpsis*; see Chapter 10) of the gods is of a blessed and immortal being (*Ep. Men.* 123–4; Cic. *Nat. D.* I 45). On this basis, the Epicureans are able to criticize the views of most people regarding the gods as impious falsehoods. Feeling anger and giving trouble to others are signs of weakness inconsistent with blessedness (*KD* 1). So Epicurus would be on firm ground in criticizing "gods" like Hera, whose jealous anger at Zeus' infidelities makes her vengefully strike out at his poor paramours, and Yahweh, who orders Joshua and his army to kill all of the men, women, children and animals in Jericho and then gets angry when they keep some of the plunder for themselves against his orders. Less plausibly, the Epicureans criticize the providential god of the Stoics, who administers (and is identical to) the cosmos, by saying that world-management is high-stress, hard work (Cic. *Nat. D.* I 52).

So it is obvious what the gods are *not* for the Epicureans, but what they *are* is much less clear. Our ancient sources seem to conflict with one another. Broadly speaking, there are two theories on what the Epicureans' gods are like, both in the ancient sources we have and in the recent scholarly literature on the topic, the "realist" and "idealist" views. As will become clear, I find the "idealist" view far more plausible. But it is worth presenting both, in part because the attractions of the "idealist" view are much clearer after working through the "realist" view.

The "realist" view: the gods are immortal extraterrestrials

The gods are supposed to be immortal and blessed. Furthermore, they are supposed to have no impact whatsoever on the workings of our (or any other) world. So, writes Lucretius, the abodes of the gods cannot be anywhere in our world. The gods are intangible to us, as we perceive them with only our minds and not our senses, and their habitation must be as tenuous as are their bodies (*DRN* V 146–55). Anywhere in *our* world, the gods would be subject to the same forces that work for our dissolution, and which trouble our bodies. Lucretius writes instead that they live in perfect peace, far removed from our world (*DRN* II 646–51), in calm, radiant realms with no storms, frosty snow or other disturbances (*DRN* III 18–22). The only place that fits these descriptions, on the "realist" view, would be the *intermundia*, the spaces in between the worlds. Here, the gods can live eternally and in perfect peace.

One's first reaction to this theory may be that it is deeply wacky: do the Epicureans seriously believe that there are races of immortal people floating in outer space? That is my own reaction, but an incredulous stare is not much of an objection. The theory, however, *is* subject to objections beyond the incredulous stare.

The first, and most serious objection is that *all* compound bodies eventually fall apart, and this would apply to the gods also. Compound bodies have void spaces in them that allow the constituents of them to be forced apart (*DRN* I 526–39). Only three things can exist eternally: (i) impenetrable elements that can repel blows, that is, individual atoms; (ii) things that are immune to blows, that is, void, which simply allows objects through it and so cannot be "hit"; and (iii) things that have no surrounding empty space into which their constituents may disperse, that is, the universe considered as a whole (*DRN* III 806–18). Lucretius lists these three things in order to show that the mind, which satisfies none of these three conditions, is not immortal. But the gods also would not satisfy them. It might be replied that the gods, living in the *intermundia*, would not be subject to the buffeting forces that break apart other compound bodies. But this reply does not work. The atoms that make up compound bodies are in constant, buzzing motion, so *internal* forces would still be at work to break apart the bodies of the gods. For the gods to be eternal, they would have to be in environments that somehow eternally replenish exactly what their bodies lose as a result of their internal vibrations.

A second set of objections comes from Epicurean biology. The Epicureans insist that the gods must be human in shape, because the gods are beautiful, and nothing can be more beautiful than a human being (Cic. *Nat. D.* I 47–8). But human beings do not just happen to have the bodily shape that they do. Instead, the bodily parts we have are well adapted for survival and reproduction in our environment. The Epicureans disagree with Aristotle's contention that hands are made *for grasping*; instead, they happen to be useful for that purpose. Nonetheless, it is no coincidence that we have hands with opposable thumbs, as they helped us survive, while creatures like us but without opposable thumbs were worse at grabbing bananas and died off. If the gods live in outer space, in need of nothing and facing danger from nothing, it would seem wildly improbable that they would have the same bodily shape as we would. Furthermore, Lucretius insists that fully grown creatures must come to be as the end result of a process of biological development from the proper sorts of "seeds", which is inconsistent with the idea of eternally existing animals like the gods.

The "idealist" view: the gods are thought-constructs

Given the serious problems with thinking that the gods literally exist as immortals in the spaces between the worlds, there is good reason on grounds of charity to see if there is another plausible way to interpret the Epicurean theory. Fortunately, there is.[1]

Where do we get our ideas of the gods? Many sources confirm that we view the gods not with our sense-organs, but with the intellect (Cic. *Nat. D.* I 49; *DRN* VI 68–79). That is, some of our ideas arise directly from sensing examples of the item in question, for example the concept of "cow" arises from seeing Bessie, Daisy, Clover and so on. But not all of our ideas are like this, and these include some of our preconceptions, such as "truth" and "usefulness". "God" is in this latter category.

Sextus Empiricus gives the most complete explanation of how the process is supposed to work (*Math.* IX 43–7, LS 23F). We start from dream impressions of human-shaped images. (This starting-point fits with the Epicureans' truly unfortunate theory [*DRN* IV 722–822] that imagination is a matter of the mind "tuning in" to some of the fine *eidōla* that are constantly impinging directly on the mind, bypassing the senses.) The Epicureans then explain how we get from this idea of "human-shaped animal" to the idea of "god" by analogy to how we get the idea of "Cyclops". Both involve "transition". In the case of a Cyclops we start with the basic idea of a human being, enlarge him, and subtract an eye. Voilà! There's a Cyclops. For the gods, we start with the idea of a happy and long-lived human being, then intensify and make perfect his happiness, and extend his lifespan endlessly. In the case of gods, however, this process of concept-formation occurs naturally and automatically, among all people.

On the "idealist" view, the gods just are such idealizations of the most blessed human life. That the gods are simply thought-constructs and not solid bodies is supported by Cicero's description of the gods' nature (Cic. *Nat. D.* I 49). We do not perceive the gods as we perceive solid bodies, which offer resistance to our touch and are perceived by the senses. Instead, our intellect attends to innumerable similar images of the gods, and these images flow *to* the gods. Some editors have wished to emend this text to the more expected sentence that the images flow *from* the gods. But if we retain the manuscript reading, this gives us the surprising but satisfying notion that the gods just are the result of this process of gathering together these images. The gods exist, but as projected ideals of human perfection. Rather than the gods creating us, we create the gods.

Thinking of the gods as thought-constructs would allow the Epicureans to retain the traditional anthropomorphic conception of the gods in the face of attacks by people such as the Presocratic Xenophanes. Xenophanes notes that the Ethiopians have black and snub-nosed gods, while the Thracians have blue-eyed, red-haired ones (Clement *Miscellanies* 7.22.1 = DK 21 B16), and he goes on to claim that if they had hands, horses would draw images of gods like horses and cattle like cattle (Clement *Miscellanies* 5.109.3 = DK 21 B16). The Epicureans can cheerfully accept this point. If the gods are our idealizations of blessedness, then we can unapologetically assert such things as: the gods have human shape because we consider that shape most beautiful of all. On the realist view, insisting that the gods in the *intermundia* must have a human shape because that shape comports with our standards of beauty (as opposed to, for example, Martian standards) seems to be a piece of absurd parochialism.

The Epicurean spokesman in *De Natura Deorum* also claims that even though the gods have human appearance, they have not bodies but "quasi-bodies", and they have not blood but "quasi-blood" (Cic. *Nat. D.* I 48–9). Cicero dutifully records the Epicurean doctrine in his exposition of the theory, but later he admits he has no idea what the Epicureans mean by "quasi-body" and "quasi-blood", and he mocks the idea as a piece of obscure flimflam (Cic. *Nat. D.* I 71). But asserting that a god has a "quasi-body" may be a sensible way to try to answer the difficult question of whether a god has a body. Either straightforward answer seems wrong. The Epicurean would not want to answer that a god does *not* have a body. After all, the idea of a god is an idea of a supremely blessed being that is human in form: that is, an idea of a being with a body. And the Epicurean would not want to give the impression that a god is simply incorporeal void, or some sort of disembodied intelligence like Plato's deity of cosmic mind, such as the Craftsman of the *Timaeus*. But nor does a god, as a thought-construct, have a body in the same way as does George W. Bush. Formed by us from streams of images, a god would be *atomic* in some sense (as are all mental phenomena), but he is not a solid body that offers resistance to blows, as does George W. Bush. Similarly, the idea of a god would be an idea of a being with blood, but a god does not have blood in the same way as does George W. Bush.

A similar manoeuvre may help to explain away some of the passages that suggest a home for the gods in the *intermundia*. We can ask "Do the gods have an abode?", and in one sense, of course, the answer should be yes: since our idea of the gods is an idea of supremely blessed beings with human form, this would include the idea of living *somewhere*. But the gods will not have an abode in our world, in the way in which George W. Bush has a ranch outside Waco. This is for two reasons: (i) since the gods are supremely blessed, they would have to live in a place free from all conditions, such as tornados, excessive heat, great humidity and so on, which cause bodily discomfort, unlike Waco or anywhere else in our world; (ii) since the gods are thought-constructs, they do have literal abodes in places such as Waco, unlike George W. Bush. It would only be by noticing reason (i) but ignoring reason (ii) that an Epicurean would want to find a literal location (like the *intermundia*) for the gods rather than simply describing the *sort* of abode the gods must inhabit.

The Epicureans make a pair of claims about the gods that, on the surface, seem contradictory. On the one hand, the gods are not affected by weakness or gratitude, and they cause us no troubles (*KD* 1). The gods are utterly indifferent to us. On the other hand, the greatest harms come from the gods to bad people and the greatest benefits to the good (*Ep. Men.* 124). But the two are consistent. As our ethical ideals, the gods can greatly benefit or harm us, even though the correct conception of the gods is of blessed beings who take no notice of us.

Consider the man who worships a jealous and vengeful god who demands blood and plunder. Of course, there really is no such god. But the belief in this kind of god causes great fear. Even more fundamentally, considering such a being worthy of worship is an expression of a disturbing psychic illness, of a misguided adoration of power and cruel domination, and belief in this god reinforces the illness. So this man's god does cause him the greatest harm.

The Epicurean joins in public celebrations of the gods because they are the cause of many good things (Phld. *Piet.* 105, IG I-56). But in these celebrations, the Epicurean does not engage in petitionary prayer or hope in some other way to curry favour from the gods, thereby gaining their help. Instead, her ideas about the gods express and help reinforce correct ideas about blessedness, and by prayerfully reflecting on and striving to emulate them, she gains the greatest benefits from her gods.

Whether one accepts the "realist" or "idealist" view, the practical upshot of Epicurean theology is identical. The gods function as ethical ideals whose lives we can worship and strive to emulate, but whose wrath we need not fear. In fact, a wise Epicurean, in attaining blessedness, lives like a god among mere human beings (*Ep. Men.* 135, LS 23J). Epicureans who deify themselves in this way can, in turn, become role models for those who follow. As we have seen (Ch. 13, § "Philosophy"), Epicurus himself was regarded as this sort of human deity by later Epicureans.

SEVENTEEN

Death

Even more than fear of the gods, the fear of death troubles us. The Epicureans offer two main arguments against the fear of death: the "no subject of harm" argument and the "symmetry" argument. Both try to show that your death is not bad for you, and hence it should not be feared. But the Epicureans also address whether you should worry about your death being bad for others, or the death of others bad for you. Finally, they realize that the fear of death is often fuelled by subconscious factors, and completely curing the fear of death requires that these too be eradicated.

The "no subject of harm" argument

The main Epicurean argument against the fear of death is the "no subject of harm" argument. In it, the Epicureans argue that for death to be bad, it must be bad *for* somebody: the harm of death must have a subject. But death is annihilation: after you die, you do not exist. So your death cannot be bad for you. As Epicurus says, death is "nothing to us". When we exist, death is not present, and when death is present, we do not exist. So it is nothing, to either the living or the dead. It does not affect the living, as they are not yet dead: they have not been annihilated. And the dead do not exist, so death cannot be bad for them (*Ep. Men.* 125). As Lucretius notes in his presentation of the argument (*DRN* III 861–9), a person must exist in order for evil to befall him.

And if your death is not bad for you, it is irrational to fear it. It is rational to fear something only if it is bad, for example my fearing the wisdom tooth extraction by an incompetent dentist. As Epicurus puts it, the person who says that he fears death, not because it will be painful when it arrives but because it is painful when it is still to come, is a fool (*Ep. Men.* 125). So the Epicurean hope is that the "no subject of harm" argument will convince you that your death is not bad for you, with the consequence that you will come to realize that your fear of death is irrational. And then, realizing that your fear is irrational will cause you to shed it.

The argument, of course, rests on the assumption that death is annihilation. But the Epicureans do not simply assume this, but argue at great length that the mind is a bodily organ that dies along with the rest of the body. A person who does not know this would have reason to fear death, as he worries that he may be sent to spend an eternity in a flaming tomb with other heretics, reincarnated as a factory-farmed chicken or suffer some other horrible fate. Furthermore, it addresses only the fear that *your* death is bad for *you*. It does not address the fear that your death may be bad for your children, or that your friend's death may be bad for you. This feature does not make the argument unsuccessful, but merely limited in its scope, and the Epicureans do have some resources for soothing these latter fears of death. Also, they might assert – cynically but plausibly – that it is the fear that *your own* death is bad for *you* that is mainly responsible for anxiety. Finally, the argument concerns the badness of *death*, not of the process of dying: of being trapped in a burning car, ripped apart by wild dogs, and the like. Certain manners of dying can be extremely painful, and the Epicureans would have to concede that these would be bad for you. However, this is really a fear of *pain*, not of death, and would be handled by their overall ethics: in particular, by the assertion that severe pains are usually short-lived and often followed by death, which is not painful.

Of all parts of Epicureanism, the arguments against the fear of death have spurred the greatest interest among contemporary philosophers. Thomas Nagel's short paper "Death" is the starting-point for much of the subsequent discussion, so here I shall focus on it. Nagel's main complaint against the Epicureans is that they misidentify why we think death is bad. According to Nagel, the Epicureans argue as if we suppose that the state of non-existence is in itself bad. Nagel agrees with the Epicureans that non-existence cannot in itself be bad. But if it were the permanent cessation of consciousness in itself that we feared, we would also regard temporary periods of unconsciousness such as dreamless sleep as bad, which we do not (Nagel 1979: 3).

Instead, says Nagel, what makes death bad is what it *deprives* us of: life, and all of the goods of life. If I step out of my office tomorrow on to Peachtree Street, and a passing bus pulverizes me, then I miss out on the joys of watching my children grow up, nestling with my wife on the back porch and hanging out with my friends. So what makes getting hit by the bus bad for me is that it deprives me of all of these goods that I would have had if I had not died. There can be cases where a person's future prospects are so dim – for example a bitter, friendless man suffering from pancreatic cancer – that death is not an evil. But usually life is a good thing, and so having it taken away from you is bad (*ibid.*: 1–2).

Lucretius has a ready reply to this line of argument. Death removes both goods such as friends and family and the craving for them (*DRN* III 894–903). A *life* without these sorts of things would be bad, but the dead person does not miss them. And since the deprivation does not bother him, it does not hurt him.

This sort of reply might make it seem that the Epicureans' argument against the badness of death depends on their hedonism. Lucretius asserts that being deprived of family cannot be bad for you if you do not miss them. Likewise, Epicurus asserts in *Letter to Menoeceus* 124 that all good and bad consist in sense-experience, and death is the privation of sense-experience. If we deny the Epicureans' hedonism, we can expand the range of possible harms.

Nagel explicitly denies that hedonism is true, because we care about things other than our states of consciousness. For instance, I want for my wife and children *actually* to love me. If my wife is carrying on a torrid affair during my office hours while laughing at my cluelessness, and my children are pretending to like me in order to come into a vast inheritance while anonymously spreading around nasty stories about me on the internet, then I am not getting what I want. If I never discover their betrayals, they will never bother me. But it is mistaken to regard the betrayals as bad only because they will cause me pain if discovered. Instead, I would find discovering the betrayals so painful because I regard them as bad; that is, because I want my children and wife really to love me and be faithful to me. So even on the simple analysis of good and bad as consisting, respectively, in getting what you want and not getting what you want, unknown betrayals can be bad. Likewise, being deprived of life and the goods of life can be bad for me, even if the deprivation does not bother me (*ibid.*: 5).

It is not quite so obvious, however, that the Epicureans' argument against the badness of death depends on their hedonism. The crucial manoeuvre that Nagel makes is to admit the existence of what we might call "counterfactual harms": things that are not bad in themselves but are bad because of what would have been had they not occurred. But once we admit such harms, hedonists could also say that death is harmful, in so far as it deprives a person of pleasures he would otherwise have experienced, and hence makes him worse off.

For a follower of Bentham, this is especially obvious: longer time allows me to accumulate a greater amount of pleasure. And Nagel, although no hedonist, follows this basic line of thought when it comes to the value of life: in so far as life is something good, more of it is better (*ibid.*: 9–10). As we have seen (Ch. 12, § "Varieties of pleasure"), Epicurus rejects this conception of pleasure. Once we have reached the limit of pleasure, which is the removal of all pain in mind and body, time does not increase pleasure. So infinite time and finite time contain equal pleasure (*KD* 19). Furthermore, once you obtain the things that remove the pain caused by desire, your whole life is complete (*KD* 21). So the life of the Epicurean sage who has reached the state of *ataraxia* is complete. Since he enjoys his life, he is happy to continue living, but continuing to live does not fundamentally make his life any better, and he loses nothing when he dies.[1]

Still, if we admit such counterfactual harms, it seems that even Epicurus would have to admit that some people are harmed by death. Imagine a misguided politician, struggling to hold on to power, who is also worried about being sent to Acheron. He reads Lucretius and is attracted by his message, and he realizes that his present life is troubled. He seeks out the local Epicurean community and starts to spend time there, admiring the tranquillity of the people he meets. His life is still harried, but he resolves to work through Epicurus' *On Nature*, to see if the answers he seeks are there. But shortly before he is going to look at the arguments for why death is annihilation, he steps out of his office, and a passing horse tramples him to death. In his case, at least, it looks as though death harmed him: if the horse had not trampled him, he would have attained *ataraxia*, with just a little more time to work on his desires and to embrace Epicurus' healing message, but he did not.

But Epicurus could simply restate the basic "no subject of harm" argument in this case too. The politician's death did not affect him while he was alive, as it had not occurred yet, so it was not bad for him while he was alive, and after he died he does not exist, so it is not bad for him then either. His vain and empty desire for power and his belief in Acheron harmed him while he was alive, and his early death prevented him from curing himself, but his death still was not bad for him, as he did not exist after his death to be harmed. Paradoxically, as third-person observers, we can look back on the politician's life as a whole and say that it was worse than it would have been had he not been trampled, but for the politician living his life, there is never a point at which he is harmed by death.

This leads to Nagel's second main contention: trying to locate the exact time when the harm of death occurs is mistaken. Death is bad *for the person who died*, in so far as he is the one who is deprived of life and all of the goods of life. This may seem to involve some sort of objectionable backwards causation: how can I be harmed in 2009 by an event that has not yet occurred? But in so far as my life as a whole is rendered worse by the bus pulverizing me, it is bad for me and harms me, although not at any time in particular (Nagel 1979: 5–7).[2]

The symmetry argument

The Epicureans assume that it is mainly the possibility of post-mortem suffering that fuels the fear of death. Still, many people also find the prospect of permanent non-existence unsettling. I now exist. But one day, whether by bus, pancreatic cancer or something else, I will die. And then I will not exist. Ten years after I die, I still will not exist. And a hundred years, a thousand years, for ever and ever: an eternity of non-existence, stretching forward endlessly, awaits.

Fortunately, says Lucretius, nature has provided a mirror to allow us to contemplate what that eternity of post-mortem non-existence will be like: the eternity of pre-natal non-existence (*DRN* III 972–7). After all, there was an eternity of time before our births in which we did not exist. And when we think back on that time, we do not regard it with horror. We do not say to ourselves, "Oh my god – non-existence was so terrible! I'm lucky to have escaped it, for at least a brief time. But with death, alas, I will slip back into that wretched non-existence". Really, it was not all that bad. And we should face the prospect of our post-mortem non-existence with equal equanimity, as in all relevant respects the two are the same.

In theory, one could respond to Lucretius by agreeing that the two periods are the same, but arguing that we ought to bring our attitudes toward them in line with one another by starting to regard our pre-natal non-existence with horror. But most people who object to Lucretius grant him the supposition that we do and should regard the eternity of time before our births with equanimity. Instead, they argue that birth and death are importantly asymmetrical, so that we are rational to have differing attitudes towards each.

This is what Nagel does. Death is bad because of the goods it deprives us of. But birth does not deprive us of goods in the same sort of way. It might be asked why this is the case. After all, if my death in

2010 is bad for me because of all of the goods I would have enjoyed had I died in 2030, why is my birth in 1968 not bad for me, as it deprived me of all of the goods I would have enjoyed had I been born in 1948 instead, such as listening to Jimi Hendrix at Altamont?

People often ask silly counterfactual questions about their lives, such as "What would my life have been like if I had been born in the Middle Ages?", and then they argue over whether they would have been hailed as geniuses or burned at the stake as heretics. The correct answer is that anybody born in the Middle Ages would not have been *you*, but another person. (On the other hand, we can sensibly ask what would have happened to Jimi Hendrix had he not overdosed when he did.) Leaving aside cases of slight premature birth, you had to have been born when you were in order to be *you* (Nagel 1979: 7–8).

At least two different sorts of justification can be given for this position. The first is put forward by Saul Kripke (1980: lecture III). There are many different lives you could have led, but in order for it to be *your* life, and not the life of another human being, the same egg and sperm must have united to produce you. So the biological origin of your life is necessary as the start of *your* life, even though many possible futures branch off from this starting-point.

The second is inspired by Derek Parfit's (1971; 1984: pt III) account of personal identity. What makes me the person I am now is that I have certain beliefs, desires and character traits. And what makes me the same person across time are the bonds of psychological continuity and connectedness between my present self and past selves, especially (although not exclusively) through memory. So if "I" had been born at any time other than when I was, "my" life would have been so utterly different that it would not have been *mine* in any significant sense, but that of another person. Even if, under some science fiction scenario, the sperm and egg that united to form me had been harvested earlier and united five years prior to when I was born, the resultant person would not have been me, in a Parfitian sense. In fact, we can make the same basic point without science fiction. My parents – my adoptive parents – adopted me when I was about six months old. In Kripke's sense, there is another possible world in which Tim O'Keefe was adopted by different parents, although in that world he would not be named Tim O'Keefe, but (let us say) Dirk Dragovic. But by Parfit's standards, even though that human being could have been adopted by different people, when I look back at it now, Dirk's life is not a life that *I* could have led, but the life of a different person, as it would be so completely different in almost every particular that makes my life *my* life.

So the symmetry argument seems to succeed in so far as it shows that there is nothing fearful in eternal non-existence as such, past or future. But if one is attracted to Nagel's contention that death is bad because of what it deprives us of, there still seems to be an important asymmetry between birth and death.

The deaths of others and the effects of your death on others

As we have noted, the main Epicurean arguments against the fear of death address you fearing that your death will be bad for you. But the Epicureans do address the deaths of others and the effect of our death on other people. As strict psychological and ethical egoists, we might expect them to take a hard line concerning these: after I am dead, the welfare of my family is nothing to me, and the death of my friend is not *my* problem, except in so far as it has an impact on how he can provide for my welfare. But, consistently or not, they do not take this crass and cold-hearted line.

In so far as the main Epicurean arguments show that death is not bad for the person who has died, they should also help greatly lessen our grief at the deaths of loved ones. Most people would feel terrible if their daughter were to die during open-heart surgery or their friend were to be obliterated in a car crash. But as Lucretius notes (*DRN* III 904–11), if death is not bad for the person who has died, and the dead feel no pain whatsoever, for us to feel great pain on their behalf seems irrational.

While realizing that death is not bad for the person who has died might help reduce our grief, it does not eliminate the impact the absence of loved ones has on us. Still, even though a wise Epicurean benefits from his friends, he should have a network of friends such that the death of one of them will not ruin his life. Epicurus says that the memory of a dead friend is sweet (Plut. *Non posse* 1105e, IG I-121). This goes along with the general Epicurean recommendation to experience mental pleasures by calling up memories of past good times: when my friend has died, I should fondly and gratefully think back on him. And as a good friend and a just person, a wise Epicurean will scrupulously make whatever provisions he needs to in order to ensure the well-being of his loved ones after he dies. Indeed, Epicurus himself did so in his will.[3]

Despite all of this, the Epicureans apparently say that to eliminate entirely pain, tears and lamentations at the deaths of friends would be a kind of bad insensitivity. These pains are worth experiencing in order to seem tender and gain the benefits of friendship (Plut. *Non posse* 1101a–b, IG I-40). Here, it is hard to see why it would be good to experience pain at the deaths of friends for the sake of cultivating friendship – Plutarch even mentions weeping copiously and swooning – rather than its being good to risk great pain in order to benefit one's living friends for the sake of cultivating friendship. Likewise, the Epicurean Philodemus says that it is natural to shed a tear and feel a "bite" of sorrow at the thought that people you love will face material hardship because of your death (Phld. *On Death* XXV 2–10). These "bites" are genuine, painful emotions, but they are passing and are not severe enough to threaten seriously the overall state of tranquillity of the sage.[4] But this position might not be orthodox: as noted above (Ch. 15, § "A heterodox account of friendship"), Philodemus is probably one of the heterodox "timid" Epicureans in Cicero's *On Ends* who advance a theory of friendship in which, with familiarity, you come to love your friend for his own sake. A person who does develop this sort of other-regarding love for friends and family might be expected to feel a bite of pain at the thought that they might suffer from his death, even if it could have no impact on him directly.

The psychological complexity of the fear of death

The Epicureans believe that their arguments succeed in showing that the fear of death is irrational, and that accepting these arguments will help move you towards a state of psychic health. Still, they have no illusions that an argument or two, no matter how clever, will immediately cure the fear of death. The fear of death is a complex phenomenon, and maybe only the wise Epicurean will be free of it entirely.

The Epicureans acknowledge the existence of subconscious mental states, especially when it comes to death. For example, Lucretius discusses our attitudes towards our corpses. Many people worry about their bodies slowing putrefying, or being burned up, or being torn apart by wild animals. Lucretius says that people who have these sorts of worries may emphatically declare that they will feel nothing when they are dead, but deep in their hearts they still have the unconscious belief that some part of them survives their death to suffer (*DRN* III 870–93). Likewise, the fear of death can manifest itself in ways that the person himself does not recognize as being caused by the fear of death. Lucretius gives a vivid description of a restless man, bored at his spacious mansion, rushing off to his country villa, only to find he is no better off there. Lucretius writes that his restlessness and dissatisfaction are caused by his fear of death. He does not realize that he is engaging in the fruitless attempt to escape from himself, and that he hates himself because he is sick and does not understand the cause of his illness. What such a person needs to do first is to study the nature of things (*DRN* III 1053–75).

But if the fear of death can express itself in unexpected ways, such as restless pacing through the halls of one's mansion, the process can work the other way too: other types of psychic illness express themselves through our fear of death, so perhaps it is only the person who is entirely healthy who will be entirely free of the fear of death. Certain unjustified and destructive attitudes towards life fuel the fear of death. Lucretius depicts a personified Nature as chastising an old man for his fear of death. According to Nature, he fears death because he always desires what is not there (*DRN* III 957), and because he thinks that he has not had enough out of life. Thus, since he thinks that his life is incomplete (*DRN* III 958), he is fearful when he thinks of it being taken away from him. In his own voice, Lucretius makes much the same point at the end of book three: acquisitive attitudes and the fear of death are closely entwined. Many people are never satisfied with what they presently have. This causes them to lust for life, in order to get what they do not yet have, but this gaping thirst can never be quenched (*DRN* III 1076–86). So even if a person accepts the conclusion that death is "nothing to us", this would not immediately remove the acquisitive attitudes that cause him (inconsistently) to continue to fear death and cling to life. For that to happen, the complete Epicurean cure is needed.[5]

Lucretius also writes that the afterlife tortures of mythology are really just projections of torments that afflict people here and now (*DRN* III 978–1023). For example, there is no literal Sisyphus, condemned to push his rock to the top of a mountain, only to see it repeatedly roll back down to the bottom. But real-world politicians thirsty for public approval are like Sisyphus, as they suffer great hardships in the pursuit of power, in the end always to come away disappointed. Lucretius catalogues the real-world analogues of those mythologically tormented in Hades, and he concludes, "Hell exists here on earth – in the lives of fools" (*DRN* III 1023).

Realizing that hell is here allows us to focus our energies where we should: away from the empty torments of superstition and towards eradicating the desires that make our earthly lives hellish. Likewise, Epicurus writes, realizing that there are no afterlife blessings or torments frees us to concentrate on attaining blessedness in our ephemeral lives here and now: "We are born only once, and we cannot be born twice; and one must for all eternity exist no more. You are not in control of tomorrow and yet you delay your opportunity to rejoice" (*SV* 14, IG trans.).

Glossary of terms

aponia Lack of bodily distress. Considered the limit of bodily pleasure by the Epicureans.

apraxia Inaction. The Epicureans would often deploy *apraxia* arguments ("inaction" or "lazy" arguments), alleging that their opponents' positions (such as determinism and scepticism) would make action irrational or impossible.

ataraxia Lack of mental turmoil; tranquillity or peace of mind. Considered the limit of mental pleasure by the Epicureans, and the primary constituent of the happy life.

atom Unsplittable building-blocks of matter.

canon (*kanōn*) Literally "measuring rod", the Epicurean term for the criteria of truth.

cosmos An ordered world-system: the earth, sun, moon and other celestial bodies. For the Epicureans, our particular *cosmos* is only one of an infinite number of *cosmoi*.

cradle argument "Cradle" arguments use observations of infant behaviour to establish what is desirable. The Epicurean version claims that infant behaviour establishes that only pleasure is intrinsically desirable.

eidōla (images) Streams of atoms constantly thrown off of the surfaces of objects that cause visual sensations when they strike our eyes.

katastematic pleasures "Static" pleasures that have to do with being in a state free of want or need, such as being satiated after having eaten.

kinetic pleasures Pleasures that have to do with experiencing an enjoyable "motion", such as the sensation of eating something when hungry.

minima Smallest spatial magnitudes, which cannot even theoretically be divided further. Posited by the Epicureans to solve Zeno of Elea's paradoxes of motion.

physics The study of nature (*phusis*). For the Epicureans, "physics" includes subjects such as the basic constituents of the world and the principles that govern their movement, cosmology, biology and the relationship of the mind to the body.

preconception (*prolēpsis*) Basic concept whose meaning we grasp without need for any additional definition.

swerve An undetermined atomic motion to the side by exactly one spatial minimum. Supposedly necessary for there to be atomic collisions and for freedom of action.

teleological explanation A *telos* is something's goal, end or purpose, and teleological explanations appeal to such things as the purpose of the heart or the intentions of the gods. With the exception of appealing to the desires of animals, Epicureans generally oppose teleological explanations.

virtue A perfection of character (such as courage) or intellect (such as wisdom) that allows us to live well. The Epicureans controversially hold that they are valuable only instrumentally, for their contribution to pleasure, and not for their own sake.

void (*kenon*) Absolutely empty space.

Notes

Preface

1. B. Inwood & L. Gerson, *Hellenistic Philosophy: Introductory Readings*, 2nd edn (Indianapolis, IN: Hackett, 1997) [IG] includes, in addition to its reading on Epicureanism, extensive selections of texts on Stoicism and Scepticism, which I occasionally refer to. However, for those who want only the texts on Epicureanism, an even cheaper alternative is their *The Epicurus Reader: Selected Writings and Testimonia* (Indianapolis, IN: Hackett, 1994), which has all and only the Epicureanism texts from IG. The numbering is identical, except that *The Epicurus Reader* does not include the preface number "I", which is used in IG to indicate that those texts are in the Epicureanism section. For example, (IG I-151) is also text 151 in *The Epicurus Reader*. Volume one of A. A. Long & D. N. Sedley, *The Hellenistic Philosophers* (Cambridge: Cambridge University Press, 1987) [LS] contains the texts in English translation, along with commentary, while volume two has the Greek and Latin texts. IG has the advantages of being cheaper and of keeping together texts such as the *Letter to Menoeceus*, which are broken up into chunks and scattered here and there in LS. However, because LS groups texts by subject and includes extensive commentary on those texts, it is often easier to follow what is going on than in IG.

1. Introduction: the life of Epicurus and the history of Epicureanism

1. For readers interested in more information on the history of Epicureanism, I recommend *The Cambridge Companion to Epicureanism*, J. Warren (ed.) (Cambridge: Cambridge University Press, 2009), chapters 1 ("The Athenian Garden", D. Clay), 2 ("Epicureanism in the Roman Republic", D. Sedley), 3 ("Epicureanism

in the Roman Empire", M. Erler) and 15 ("Epicureanism in the Early Modern Period", C. Wilson).

2. Easily the best-preserved treatise of Philodemus is *On Sign Inference* (in *Philodemus, On Methods of Inference*, 2nd edn, P. De Lacey & E. De Lacey [trans.] [Naples: Bibliopolis, 1978]), although we have scholarly editions of many other (more fragmentary) treatises, such as *On Piety* and *On Frank Criticism.* V. Tsouna, *The Ethics of Philodemus* (Oxford: Oxford University Press, 2007) does a nice job of gathering together much of what Philodemus has to say about ethics. See M. Smith, (ed. & trans.), *Diogenes of Oinoanda: The Epicurean Inscription* (Naples: Bibliopolis, 1993) for most of the inscriptions of Diogenes of Oinoanda, and his "Excavations at Oinoanda: the New Epicurean Texts", *Anatolian Studies* **48** (1998), 125–70, for a few additional inscriptions. See D. Sedley, *Lucretius and the Transformation of Greek Wisdom* (Cambridge: Cambridge University Press, 1998) for an excellent extended argument that Lucretius was an Epicurean "fundamentalist" who worked directly from Epicurus' *On Nature* in composing *De Rerum Natura*, so that subsequent developments in Epicureanism had no impact on the poem.
3. I shall not discuss them here. However, for interested readers, very brief (one- or two-sentence) descriptions of most of the sources that will subsequently be referred to can be found in the "Index of Sources" in LS vol. 1, 492–500.

2. Atoms and void

1. Zeno devised variants on the same basic argument: the Stadium (reported in Aristotle, *Physics* 239b11 and *Topics* 160b7 [DK 29 A25]), and Achilles and the Tortoise (Aristotle *Physics* 239b14–18 [DK 29 A26]). I basically follow the argument as given in the Stadium.
2. Whether Epicurus himself drew all of these conclusions, or whether some were drawn by later Epicureans, is not clear: see the commentary in LS §11 for more discussion.
3. See G. Cambiano, "Philosophy, Science and Medicine", in *The Cambridge History of Hellenistic Philosophy*, K. Algra (ed.), 585–613 (Cambridge: Cambridge University Press, 1999), 587–90, for more on this topic.

3. Atomic motion

1. Whether Democritus thinks atoms have weight is unclear. Our sources are inconsistent; some have him attributing weight to them, while others explicitly deny it and say that weight is an Epicurean innovation. The usual way of reconciling these inconsistent reports is to say that having "weight" in the sense of a natural motion of direction *is* an Epicurean innovation, and that atoms have "weight" for Democritus in some other sense: either a tendency to move towards

the centre of our cosmos when inside the cosmic vortex (the majority view), or in the sense closer to the modern concept of "mass"; D. O'Brien, *Theories of Weight in the Ancient World: Four Essays on Democritus, Plato and Aristotle. A Study in the Development of Ideas. Volume One: Democritus, Weight and Size: An Exercise in the Reconstruction of Early Greek Philosophy* (Paris: Les Belles Lettres, 1981). See D. Furley, "Aristotle and the Atomists on Motion in a Void", in his *Cosmic Problems*, 77–90, esp. 80–81, for a good summary of the texts and the literature, and "Weight and Motion in Democritus' Theory", in *Cosmic Problems*, 91–102, for a summary of O'Brien and some pointed criticisms. Furley himself is alone in thinking that Democritus, like Epicurus, attributes to atoms a natural direction of motion; see my *Epicurus on Freedom* (Cambridge, Cambridge University Press, 2005), 120 n.28, for some criticisms.

2. See J. L. Mackie, *The Miracle of Theism* (Oxford: Clarendon Press, 1982), 92–5, for a brief discussion of this family of cosmological arguments.
3. Most scholars who evaluate the cosmogonic argument simply consider it a failure, for the reasons given above. The charitable interpretation given here is my own. My *Epicurus on Freedom*, ch. 5 (a revised version of my "Does Epicurus Need the Swerve as an *Archê* of Collisions?", *Phronesis* **41** [1996], 305–17) gives more details and argument, for those who wish to pursue the topic further or who harbour doubts about my proposal and want to see whether those doubts are justified.
4. Jeffrey Purinton coined the happy name "swerviness". See his "Epicurus on 'Free Volition' and the Atomic Swerve", *Phronesis* **44**(4) (1999), 253–99, esp. 271–2, for more on the sense in which swerves can be said to have *some* sort of cause.

4. Sensible qualities

1. Some of this chapter is adapted from my "The Ontological Status of Sensible Qualities for Democritus and Epicurus", *Ancient Philosophy* **17** (1997), 119–34, which gives further arguments in support of the interpretations of Democritus and Epicurus offered here. See T. Ganson, "Democritus against Reducing Sensible Qualities", *Ancient Philosophy* **19** (1999), 201–15, for some criticisms of that interpretation of Democritus, and D. Furley, "Democritus and Epicurus on Sensible Qualities", in *Passions and Perceptions*, J. Brunschwig & M. Nussbaum (eds), 72–94 (Cambridge: Cambridge University Press, 1993), D. Sedley, "Epicurean Anti-Reductionism", in *Matter and Metaphysics*, J. Barnes & M. Mignucci (eds), 295–327 (Naples: Bibliopolis, 1988), and R. Wardy, "Eleatic Pluralism", *Archiv für Geschichte der Philosophie* **70** (1988), 125–46, for some other alternatives.
2. Theophrastus' *De Sensibus* is our primary source for Democritus' theory of perception. Theophrastus was Aristotle's successor as head of the Lyceum.
3. For Theophrastus' discussion of the sense of taste, see *De Sensibus* 65–70.
4. See *DRN* IV 615–26 for the account of taste, *DRN* IV generally for sensation, with *DRN* IV 217–721 for each of the senses.

5. Whether Democritus thinks that knowledge is merely difficult or impossible to attain is a matter of some dispute; see R. Hankinson, *The Sceptics* (London: Routledge, 1995), 47–50, and *Cause and Explanation in Ancient Greek Thought* (Oxford: Oxford University Press, 1998), 201–5, for an introduction to some of the reports and issues regarding Democritus' scepticism, and P. Curd, "Why Democritus Was Not a Skeptic", in *Essays in Ancient Greek Philosophy, Vol. 6: Before Plato*, A. Preus (ed.), 149–69 (Albany, NY: SUNY Press, 2001) for a recent argument that Democritus is not a sceptic and references to much of the literature on this topic. Fortunately, we do not need to settle this question to understand Epicurus. Democritus certainly said many things that appear sceptical. The Epicureans viewed him as a sceptic (see *Against Colotes* 1108f), and Epicurus is interested in avoiding the sceptical difficulties that Democritus runs into by challenging Democritus' view on the unreality of sensible qualities, whether or not Democritus himself ultimately thinks that these difficulties can be overcome.

5. Cosmology

1. This phrase, and this way of organizing ancient cosmologies, comes from D. Furley, *Cosmic Problems: Essays on Greek and Roman Philosophy of Nature* (Cambridge: Cambridge University Press, 1989).
2. *De Caelo* (On the heavens) is the fullest statement of Aristotle's cosmology.

6. Biology and language

1. See fragments DK 31 B57, B60, and B61, and Aristotle *Physics* 198b–199b.
2. Stoic *lekta* are not *exactly* propositions; propositions are one species of *lekta*. Long and Sedley translates *lekta* as "sayables". "Complete" *lekta* are the meanings of statements (such as "my finger is cut"), and "incomplete" *lekta* are predicates (such as "is cut"). See LS §33 for more information.

7. The mind

1. Shortly after Epicurus' time, medical discoveries made via vivisection gave excellent evidence that the mind is located in the head, not the chest. Lucretius himself follows Epicurus and shows no awareness of these advances, but other Epicureans were aware of them. See Sedley, *Lucretius and the Transformation of Greek Wisdom*, 68–72, for more information.
2. Lucretius uses this dependence to show that the mind is not only corporeal, but also mortal.
3. Some of this section is adapted from my "Action and Responsibility", in *The*

Cambridge Companion to Epicureanism, J. Warren (ed.), 142–57 (Cambridge: Cambridge University Press, 2009).

4. These authors are discussed in J. Annas, "Epicurus on Agency", in *Passions and Perceptions: Studies in Hellenistic Philosophy of Mind, Proceedings of the 5th Symposium Hellenisticum*, J. Brunschwig & M. Nussbaum (eds) (Cambridge: Cambridge University Press, 1993), 66–9. For Hermarchus on the differences between human and animal abilities, see Porphyry *On Abstinence* I 7–12.
5. I think that the Epicureans' reading of Democritus as an eliminativist is inconsistent with too many other things he says to be rightly ascribed to him, as Democritus seems to acknowledge the existence of temporary compound bodies like *cosmoi*: see my "The Ontological Status of Sensible Qualities", 122–3, and C. Taylor, *The Atomists: Leucippus and Democritus. Fragments: A Text and Translation with a Commentary* (Toronto: University of Toronto Press, 1999), 152. The Epicureans likewise view Parmenides as eliminating all compound bodies, such as water and the cities of Europe and Asia, a reading that Plutarch disputes: see *Against Colotes* 1113f ff. (Many modern scholars would also dispute it: P. Curd, *The Legacy of Parmenides: Eleatic Monism and Later Presocratic Thought* (Princeton, NJ: Princeton University Press, 1997) is an excellent recent interpretation of Parmenides and his influence on later thinkers, and she would also disagree with Colotes.) However, it is not a lunatic reading of either Parmenides or Democritus, and some (e.g. Wardy, "Eleatic Pluralism") defend the eliminative interpretation of Democritus. R. Pasnau, "Democritus and Secondary Qualities", *Archiv für Geschichte der Philosophie* **89** (2007), 99–121, is agnostic but thinks this "radical" reading has much going for it, and he gives a thoughtful discussion of what exactly the position amounts to.
6. See my *Epicurus on Freedom*, 68–9.
7. See P. van Inwagen, *Material Beings* (Ithaca, NY: Cornell University Press, 1990) for an extended argument that no (non-biological) composite material objects exist.
8. For much more detail, see my *Epicurus on Freedom*, ch. 4. C. Atherton, "Reductionism, Rationality and Responsibility: A Discussion of Tim O'Keefe, *Epicurus on Freedom*", *Archiv für Geschichte der Philosophie* **89** (2007), 192–230, gives detailed criticisms of my interpretations of these texts.
9. See S. Laursen, "The Early Parts of Epicurus *On Nature* 25th Book", *Cronache Ercolanesi* **25** (1995), 5–109, and "The Later Parts of Epicurus *On Nature* 25th Book", *Cronache Ercolanesi* **27** (1997), 5–82, for the latest edition of *On Nature* 25. The passage discussed here is mostly from Laursen, "The Later Parts", 19–23. But much more easily accessible is an earlier version of the Greek text (LS vol. 2, 20B and 20C), translations of which can be found in LS vol. 1, 20B and 20C and IG 34.
10. This view was first advanced by David Sedley. See D. Sedley, "Epicurus' Refutation of Determinism", in *Suzètèsis: Studi sull'epicureismo greco e romano offerti a M. Gigante*, vol. I, 11–51 (Naples: Bibliopolis, 1983) and "Epicurean Anti-Reductionism" for this "radical emergence" interpretation; a shorter synopsis of the view can be found in the commentary in LS §20.

8. Freedom and determinism

1. See my *Epicurus on Freedom* for a detailed considerations of the issues treated here; some of this chapter is adapted from that book and from my "Action and Responsibility". Readers should be aware that the interpretation presented in this chapter is highly controversial, as is every interpretation of this topic.
2. C. Bailey, *The Greek Atomists and Epicurus* (New York: Russell and Russell, [1928] 1964), 838–42, and *Titi Lvcreti Cari: De Rervm Natvra: Libri Sex* (Oxford: Clarendon Press, 1947), 318–23, 433–7, Purinton, "Epicurus on 'Free Volition'", and D. Fowler, *Lucretius on Atomic Motion: A Commentary on* De rerum natura 2.1–332 (Oxford: Oxford University Press, 2002), commentary on *DRN* II 251–93 and appendix 1, all advance (roughly) this view, which is probably the most common interpretation. See my *Epicurus on Freedom*, ch. 2, for more discussion of this family of views and of *DRN* II 251–93.
3. For example, see P. Huby, "The First Discovery of the Freewill Problem", *Philosophy* **42** (1967), 353–62; LS vol. 1, 107; E. Asmis, "Free Action and the Swerve", *Oxford Studies in Ancient Philosophy* **8** (1990), 275.
4. See D. Furley, 1967. *Two Studies in the Greek Atomists* (Princeton, NJ: Princeton University Press, 1967), 163, and my *Epicurus on Freedom*, 44–6.
5. Lucretius describes the atomic basis of *voluntas* and action in book four of *DRN*, especially *DRN* IV 877–906. In his description, swerves play no direct role in the production of action. The action-theory in *DRN* IV seems "mechanistic", in the sense that, given the incoming stimulus and the state of the soul, action follows automatically. See Furley, *Two Studies in the Greek Atomists*, 210–26, and my *Epicurus on Freedom*, 37–42.
6. This terminology comes from LS vol. 1, 466.
7. Since Carneades is a sceptic, we should be careful in speaking about his positions or his beliefs. One common sceptical procedure was to advance arguments in support of a position simply in order to counterbalance the arguments for an opposing position, without the sceptic himself being committed to the argument or its conclusion. But for ease of reading, I shall simply speak of the arguments advanced by Carneades in *On Fate* as if he endorses them. Cicero, at least, seems to endorse them. See H. Thorsrud, *Ancient Scepticism* (Stocksfield: Acumen, 2008), chs 4, 5, for more on these issues.
8. This has striking similarities to modern notions of "agent causation". For an influential presentation of such a view, see R. Chisholm, "Human Freedom and the Self", reprinted in *Free Will*, G. Watson (ed.), 7–29 (Oxford: Oxford University Press, [1964] 1982).
9. David Sedley, who advances the "radical emergence" view of the self, which has similarities to Carneades' view (see Ch. 7, § "Reason and the reality of the mental"), does think that Epicurus had reason to posit the swerve. Without the swerve, the "radically emergent" self would have no "elbow room" in which to exercise its power, as the laws governing atomic motion would be sufficient to determine what occurs in my mind. But this is mistaken: if we grant that there

is a "radically emergent" self that gains causal independence from the atoms that constitute the mind, then *ex hypothesi* the basic laws that give the motions of individual atoms are not always sufficient to determine the motions of mind, as there is an additional causal factor at work.

9. Scepticism

1. This is how Myles Burnyeat puts it in "The Upside-down Back-to-front Sceptic of Lucretius IV 472", *Philologus* **122** (1978), 197–206, esp. 205. My discussion here is indebted to his.
2. What understanding the sceptics themselves have of the "plausible" is highly controversial. The term that Carneades uses here translated "plausible", *pithanon*, can go either way. The majority (but far from consensus) view is that for Carneades *pithanon* is mere subjective convincingness. On the other hand, Cicero seems to consider the plausible to be more probably true than not. See Thorsrud, *Ancient Scepticism*, chs 4, 5, for much more on these issues.
3. I radically oversimplify. Sextus includes in the sceptic's criteria of action (i) laws and customs (such as our convention that cannibalism is bad) and (ii) kinds of expertise such as medicine. But getting into how a sceptic can incorporate these additional practical criteria would take us too far afield from the topic at hand. See Thorsrud, *Ancient Scepticism*, ch. 9 for more on the life of a Pyrrhonist, and M. Burnyeat, "Can the Sceptic Live his Scepticism?", in *Doubt and Dogmatism*, J. Barnes, M. Burnyeat & M. Schofield (eds), 20–53 (Oxford: Oxford University Press, 1980) for a fascinating and influential discussion of whether Pyrrhonian Scepticism is liveable.

10. The canon

1. See Lucretius *DRN* IV 353–63 for a discussion of the square tower in the distance. I borrow the eye/camera analogy to explain the truth of impressions from Long and Sedley's commentary on the truth of all impressions; LS, vol. 1, 83–6.
2. *On Nature* 25 26–30 (LS 20C). The text is *much* less clear than my brief synopsis makes it appear. It is one of the papyri found in the Epicurean library in Herculaneum that was buried in the eruption of Mount Vesuvius, which also destroyed the town of Pompeii. The text is gappy and bristles with unexplained technical terminology. See my *Epicurus on Freedom*, 89–93, for more detail on my reading of the text.
3. Plutarch makes an objection to the Epicureans along these general lines, although it differs somewhat, in *Against Colotes* 1121c–e.

11. Pleasure, the highest good

1. *Nicomachean Ethics* I i lays out the basic framework very clearly. See J. Annas, *The Morality of Happiness* (Oxford: Oxford University Press, 1993), ch. 1, for an excellent discussion of this common ethical framework.
2. See *Nicomachean Ethics* I vii for Aristotle's famous "function argument", in which he grounds his conception of happiness in a human "function" (*ergon*) supplied by our human nature.
3. In fact the thesis applies to animals generally, not just human beings.
4. Interestingly, Torquatus notes that some Epicureans express doubts that this sort of proof was sufficient (*On Ends* I 31).
5. See Mill's proof of the principle of utility in chapter four of *Utilitarianism*.

12. Varieties of pleasure, varieties of desire

1. Indeed, Gisela Striker, "Epicurean Hedonism", in *Passions and Perceptions*, J. Brunschwig & M. Nussbaum (ed.), 3–17 (Cambridge: Cambridge University Press, 1993) (reprinted in her *Essays on Hellenistic Epistemology and Ethics*, 196–208 [Cambridge: Cambridge University Press, 1996]) argues that something like this is precisely the Epicurean position: that all pleasures (both kinetic and katastematic) are simply identical to the absence of pain. This, of courses, raises the pressing question of why Epicurus would then call them pleasures. Striker suggests that perhaps this is because any time we are aware of being in a state of painlessness, our awareness will also involve various sensory states we are undergoing.
2. J. Gosling & C. Taylor, *The Greeks on Pleasure* (Oxford: Oxford University Press, 1982), chs 18–19, first put forward something like the interpretation I sketch below, with K. Arenson, *Pleasure and the Absence of Pain: Reading Epicurus' Hedonism Through Plato's* Philebus, PhD dissertation, Emory University (2009) modifying their account in the face of objections and developing it at much greater length.
3. Porphyry, *On Abstinence* 1.51.6–52.1, LS 21J. Generally speaking, the Epicureans are hard on sexual desire. They admit sexual desire is natural, but insist that it is unnecessary because you can have a happy life without satisfying it. The Epicureans asserts that sex never helped anybody, and you should be content if at least it does no harm. The wise person will marry and have children when the circumstances indicate it, but he will not fall in love (*DL* X 118–19). Lucretius has a long, detailed and bitter polemic against romantic love (*DRN* IV 1058–1208), in which he rails against the ways in which it distorts the lover's judgement and disturbs his peace of mind.

13. The virtues and philosophy

1. In other contexts, *to kalon* can mean "the beautiful", as in the ultimate object of erotic desire in Plato's dialogue the *Symposium*.
2. Porphyry *To Marcella* 31 (IG I-124); trans. adapted from IG.
3. *Against Colotes* 1117f (IG I-125); *DRN* I 146–8, II 259–61, III 91–3, VI 39–41.
4. The following remarks are inspired by the much more extensive discussion in Nussbaum (1986), although I do not directly follow her way of framing the issue.
5. For instance, Epicurus allegedly called his erstwhile teacher Nausiphanes a "jellyfish", the followers of Plato "the toadies of Dionysius", and Aristotle a profligate who took to selling drugs after squandering his inheritance (*DL* X 8).
6. A characteristic statement of Cicero's attitude is *Academica* 2.7–9 (IG III-21, LS 68S).

14. Justice

1. This raises the question of whether human beings who are unable to enter into agreements about how to behave (such as small children and the severely mentally disabled) are included in the justice contract. On the one hand, the same reasoning that excludes non-human animals would seem to apply to them also. On the other hand, Lucretius clearly includes children when describing the first "justice contract" (*DRN* V 1011–27). The answer is probably that they cannot be *direct* parties to the contract, but they can be *indirectly* covered in so far as the parties include in their agreement standards about how to treat these other people. (Lucretius says that the first "justice contractors" claimed protection for their women and children.)
2. See Diogenes of Oinoanda fr. 56, in Smith, *Diogenes of Oinoanda*. This implies, perhaps surprisingly, that there can be justice apart from law. My own view is that such a community would still need *agreements* about how to behave in order for the members to avoid indirectly and inadvertently harming one another, but would not need any enforcement mechanism to compel adherence to that agreement. See my "Would a Society of Wise Epicureans Be Just?", *Ancient Philosophy* **21** (2001), 133–46, for more on this issue.
3. It is worth noting that many Roman Epicureans – such as Cassius, who helped assassinate Julius Caesar – ignored this advice.

15. Friendship

1. See D. O'Connor, "The Invulnerable Pleasures of Epicurean Friendship", *Greek, Roman, and Byzantine Studies* **30** (1989), 165–86, for much more on the communal nature of Epicurean friendship. In fact, O'Connor thinks that, for the

Epicureans, *philia* is better translated by "fellowship" than by the usual "friendship".

2. Philodemus col. XIXb, in *Philodemus: On Frank Criticism*, D. Kontan, D. Clay & C. Glad (ed. & trans.) (Atlanta, GA: Society of Biblical Literature, 1998). See also the editors' introduction, pp. 5-8 and 10-20, and Fr. 15, 28, 41, 43, 50, 81, and 84.
3. Cicero derides the celebrations of Epicurus' birthday in *On Ends* II 99–103. For more discussion of the details of the Epicurean communities and how they had celebrations, mugs of Epicurus and so on, see D. Clay, *Paradosis and Survival: Three Chapters in the History of Epicurean Philosophy* (Ann Arbor, MI: University of Michigan Press, 1998).
4. For instance, see P. Mitsis, *Epicurus' Ethical Theory: The Pleasures of Invulnerability* (Ithaca, NY: Cornell University Press, 1988), ch. 3, and Annas, *The Morality of Happiness*, ch. 11. The account of Epicurean friendship in this chapter is adapted from my "Is Epicurean Friendship Altruistic?", *Apeiron* **34** (2001), 269–305, which goes into the details of the texts and competing interpretations of them at more tedious length than here.
5. The Latin term here translated "love" (*diligo*), as well as the Greek term for "friendship love", *phileō*, allow for such a "behavioural" sense (see my "Is Epicurean Friendship Altruistic?", 295–7, for more). If "love" seems more difficult to interpret in such a way, substitute the word "care": in one sense, the Epicurean sage cares for his friends as much as for himself (in the sense of what he does), while in another he cares only about himself (in the sense of what he ultimately values).
6. From "Of the Dignity or Meanness of Human Nature," in David Hume, *Essays: Moral, Political, and Literary*, rev. edn (Indianapolis, IN: Liberty Fund, 1985), 85–6.
7. These thoughts regarding such apparently independent mental pleasures of friendship in Epicureanism are inspired by M. Strahm, *Epicurean Friendship: How are Friends Pleasurable?*, Master's thesis, Georgia State University (2009), which explores these issues in greater depth.

16. The gods

1. The basic line of interpretation below, plus many of the arguments in favour of it, are taken from LS §23.

17. Death

1. See J. Warren, *Facing Death: Epicurus and His Critics* (Oxford: Oxford University Press, 2004), 199–212, for an interesting discussion of the Epicureans and suicide. The Epicurean sage seems to have no positive reason to want to

continue living, since his life is complete, and so no good reason not to kill himself. Of course, as long as his life is basically pleasant, he has no good reason to kill himself either. Warren concludes that Epicureans "offer no significant positive reason for wishing to continue to live, beyond a mere inertia", which is "quite unappealing" (*ibid.*: 210).

2. Nagel argues for this by drawing an analogy to a stroke victim who is reduced to an infantile state. The victim in the infantile state is not bothered by his condition, so it does not seem quite right to say that he is being harmed at that time. Instead, if anybody is being harmed, it is the person who existed prior to the stroke, who was reduced to the infantile state by the stroke.
3. For great detail on Epicurus' will, see Warren, *Facing Death*, 161–99. Warren also argues that having the sort of concern for what occurs after one's death that goes into the writing of wills and carefully ensuring that their provisions will be carried out is inconsistent with the Epicurean position that death is "nothing to us". I am not convinced; see my review of Warren, *Facing Death* in *Ancient Philosophy* **26** (2006), 430–35.
4. See Tsouna, *The Ethics of Philodemus*, ch. 2 for more on bites in the ethics of Philodemus.
5. For more on this idea, see my "Lucretius on the Cycle of Life and the Fear of Death", *Apeiron* **36** (2003), 43–65, esp. §4.

Further reading

1. Introduction: The life of Epicurus and the history of Epicureanism

Ancient sources *DL* X 1–16 (parts of which are in IG I-1); *DRN* I 1–135. (The opening statements of purpose and eulogies to Epicurus at the beginnings of the other five books of *De Rerum Natura* are also instructive regarding the practical and evangelical cast of Epicureanism.)

For those interested in Epicureanism as a social movement and a basis as community, see Diskin Clay's "Individual and Community in the First Generation of the Epicurean School", in *Paradosis and Survival* (1998), ch. 4. For an excellent discussion of what is involved with self-identifying as a member of a philosophical movement in Hellenistic times, see David Sedley's "Philosophical Allegiance in the Greco-Roman world" (1989). Sedley argues that it involves "a virtually religious commitment to the authority of a founder figure" (*ibid.*: 119), and he shows in detail how this attitude influences the activities of later Epicureans.

2. Atoms and void

Ancient sources Epicurus *Ep. Hdt.* 38–41, 54–9, 68–73 (IG I-2 38–41, 54–9, 68–73; LS 4A, 5A, 7B, 8A, 9A, 12D); *DRN* I 146–634 (LS 4B, 4C, 5B, 6A, 7A, 8B, 9C), II 730–1022 (LS 12E); Sext. Emp. *Math.* X 219–27 (IG I-89, LS 7C), X 257 (IG I-82).

David Sedley's "Two Conceptions of Vacuum" (1982) argues that Democritus and the Epicureans actually had two very different conceptions of void: Democritus thought of void as *emptiness*, a sort of privative stuff that could move around (for instance, to fill a space previously occupied by an atom), whereas the Epicureans think void is simply unoccupied space. David Furley's "Indivisible Magnitudes" in his *Two Studies in the Greek Atomists* (1967) is a groundbreaking look at the Epicurean theory of spatial minima, and its background in Zeno, Aristotle and others.

3. Atomic motion

Ancient sources Epicurus *Ep. Hdt.* 43–4, 60–62 (IG I-2 43–4, 60–62; LS 11A, 10C, 11E); *DRN* II 184–250 (IG I-28; LS 11H); Aëtius I.3.18ff. (IG I-77).

The main topic of Walter Englert's *Epicurus on the Swerve and Voluntary Action* (1987) is the swerve's role in preserving free action. However, chapters 2 and 3 ("The Nature of the Swerve" and "The Swerve and Epicurean Physics") are good places to go for discussions of how exactly the swerve is supposed to work physically (Is it a 90 degree turn to the side, or an oblique 45 degree turn? What happens when there is a swerve by an atom that is not falling straight down?) as well as more in-depth treatments of many topics mentioned in passing here. Furley's "Aristotle and the Atomists on Motion in a Void" in his *Cosmic Problems* (1989) argues that the scholarly near-consensus on Democritus, that atoms have no natural direction of motion, is mistaken.

4. Sensible qualities

Ancient sources Epicurus *Ep. Hdt.* 68–71 (IG I-2 68-71; LS 7B); Plut. *Adv. Col.* 1109a–1112e (IG I-29; LS 16I); Polystratus *On Irrational Contempt* 23.26–26.23 (LS 7D).

David Furley's "Democritus and Epicurus on Sensible Qualities" (1993) argues that Democritus' position on sensible qualities is a result of his debt to Eleatic philosophers such as Parmenides and Melissus and that Epicurus runs into the same sceptical difficulties as Democritus despite his efforts to avoid them. I think that both these contentions are mistaken (see my "The Ontological Status of Sensible Qualities" [1997] for the reasons), but this paper is stimulating and astute, and a good point of entry for the textual and philosophical issues. Although Mi-Kyoung Lee's *Epistemology after Protagoras* (2005) deals only in passing with Epicureanism (mainly with the Epicureans' portrayals of Democritus), this book is an excellent study of the relationship between relativism and scepticism in ancient philosophy.

5. Cosmology

Ancient sources Epicurus *Ep. Hdt.* 41–5 73–4, 76–7 (IG I-2 41–5 73–4, 76–7; LS 10A, 12B, 11A, 13A); *Ep. Pyth.* 88–91 (IG I-3 88–91; LS 13B); *KD* 1 (IG I-5 1; LS

23E4); *DRN* I 1–101, 951–1051 (LS 10B), II 184–215, 1048–104 (LS 13D), V 91–613 (LS 13F, 18D), VI 160–422; Simp. *in Phys.* 203b15 (IG I-90), 198b29 (IG I-111); Lactant. *On the Anger of God* 13.20–22 (IG I-109).

David Furley's "The Greek Theory of the Infinite Universe" (1981) is a nuanced exploration of the philosophical motivations of the atomist theory of an "infinite universe", which concludes that a desire for a unified theory of motion was paramount.

6. Biology and language

Ancient sources Epicurus *Ep. Hdt.* 75–6 (IG I-2 75–6; LS 19A); *DRN* IV 823–57 (LS 13E), V 772–1090 (LS 13I, 19B, 22K); Simp. *in Phys.* 198b29 (IG I-111); Diogenes of Oinoanda 10.2.11 ff. (LS 19C).

Gordon Campbell's *Lucretius on Creation and Evolution* (2003) is a detailed commentary on *De rerum natura* V 772–1104, which deals with the origins of species, society and language. As a commentary, it deals with many textual issues on a line-by-line basis, but along the way and in its introduction it also raises many interesting philosophical questions about the doctrines and how they relate to later Darwinian theories. Alexander Verlinsky's "Epicurus and his Predecessors on the Origins of Language" (2005) is a careful, detailed, and sympathetic reconstruction of the Epicurean theory, which highlights the continuity between Epicurus' philosophy of language and his general opposition to teleology.

7. The mind

Ancient sources Epicurus *Ep. Hdt.* 63–7 (IG I-2 63–7; LS 14A); Epicurus *On Nature* XXV 19–30 (IG I-34; LS 20B, 20C); *DRN* III 94–869 (LS 14B, 14D, 14F, 14G, 14H 14J); Plut. *Adv. Col.* 1110e–1111b (IG I-29), 1116c–d.

David Sedley's "Epicurean Anti-Reductionism" (1998), as the title suggests, argues against the sort of "reductionist" interpretation of Epicurus put forward in this chapter and, as such, it has been highly influential, both in attracting supporters and in spurring opponents to articulate the case against Sedley. Robert Pasnau's "Democritus and Secondary Qualities" (2007) argues that it is anachronistic to attribute the distinction between primary and secondary qualities to Democritus and, in so doing, he opens issues of how to understand Democritus' ontology generally. It includes an excellent discussion of the Epicureans' view that Democritus is an eliminativist regarding compound bodies.

8. Freedom and determinism

Ancient sources Epicurus *Ep. Men.* 133–4 (IG I-4 133–4; LS 20A); *DRN* II 251–93 (IG I-28; LS 20F), IV 877–906 (LS 14E); Cic. *Fat.* 18–48 (IG I-15; LS 20E, 70G, 55S, 20H, 34C, 62C).

My *Epicurus on Freedom* (2005) gives more extended arguments for the (controversial) conclusions advanced in this chapter, plus pointers to much of the recent literature. James Warren's "Epicureans and the Present Past" (2006) deals with an interesting question raised by the Epicureans' treatment of statements regarding the future: what are the truth-makers for statements regarding the *past*?

9. Scepticism

Ancient sources *DRN* IV 469–521 (IG I-27; LS 16A).

Myles Burnyeat's "The Upside-down Back-to-front Sceptic of Lucretius 4.472" (1978) starts with an apparently narrow textual question: why does Lucretius describe the sceptic using the odd imagery of the sceptic not merely standing on his head, but also back to front? But in coming to an answer to that question, Burnyeat goes on to consider more broadly the way the Epicurean "self-refutation" argument against the sceptics is supposed to work.

10. The canon

Ancient sources Epicurus *Ep. Hdt.* 37–8, 49–51, 76–80 (IG I-2 37–8, 49–51, 76–80; LS 17C, 15A); *Ep. Pyth.* 85–8, 92–115 (IG I-3 85–8, 92–155; LS 18C, 13B); *KD* 23, 24 (IG I-5 23, 24; LS 16D); Epicurus *On Nature* XXV 26–30 (IG I-34; LS 20C); *DL* X 30–34 (IG I-7; LS 17A, 19I, 16B, 15F, 17E, 18B, 19J); *DRN* IV 379–499 (LS 16A, 16H), V 509–33 (LS 18D), V 592–770, VI 703–11 (LS 18E); Sext. Emp. *Math.* VII 203–16 (IG I-68; LS 18A), XIII 63–4 (IG I-70; LS 16F); Plut. *Adv. Col.* 1120d–e, 1121c–e (IG I-29).

Elizabeth Asmis's *Epicurus' Scientific Method* (1984) is the most detailed and comprehensive treatment of Epicurean epistemology available. Gisela Striker's "Epicurus on the Truth of Sense-impressions" in her *Essays on Hellenistic Epistemology and Ethics* (1996) argues that sensations are *alēthēs* in the sense of all being true, not merely real, and concludes that the theory is an interesting (if ultimately unsuccessful) attempt to find an infallible ground for knowledge.

11. Pleasure, the highest good

Ancient sources Epicurus *Ep. Men.* 129–30 (IG I-4 129–30; LS 21B); Cic. *Fin.* I 29–33 (IG I-21; LS 21A).

Jacques Brunschwig's "The Cradle Argument in Epicureanism and Stoicism" (1986) is, as the title says, a detailed examination of how examining infant behaviour is supposed to establish what the highest good is. A different analysis of the functioning of the cradle argument can be found in Sedley's "The Inferential Foundations of Epicurean Ethics" (1998), as part of a larger (and quite fruitful) discussion of the foundations of Epicurean ethics. John Cooper's "Pleasure and Desire in Epicurus", in his *Reason and Emotion* (1998), argues that Epicurus is only an *ethical* hedonist, not both an ethical and psychological hedonist. Reading this essay paired with Raphael Woolf's rebuttal "What Kind of Hedonist is Epicurus?" (2004) would be a nice introduction to the issues and texts regarding Epicurean hedonism.

12. Varieties of pleasure, varieties of desire

Ancient sources Epicurus *Ep. Men.* 127–8, 130–31 (IG I-4 127–8, 130–31; LS 21B); *KD* 3, 9, 18, 19, 29, 30 (IG I-5 3, 9, 18, 19, 29, 30; LS 21C, 21D, 23E1, 24C, 21E3); *SV* 33, 59, 69, 71 (IG I-6 33, 59, 69, 71; LS 21G1, 21G4, 21H2); *DL* X 22 (IG I-41; LS 24D), X 136–7 (IG I-9; LS 21R); *DRN* II 963–6, III 28–30, IV 858–76; Cic. *Fin.* I 37–9 (IG I-22; LS 21A), 55–7 (IG I-23; LS 21U), II 28–35; Porph. *Abst.* 1.51.6–52.1 (LS 21J).

In J. Gosling and C. Taylor's *The Greeks on Pleasure* (1982), chs 18–20 concentrate on Epicurus and make the controversial argument that Epicurus himself does not sharply distinguish between kinetic and katastematic pleasures. But the whole book is well worth reading. Jeffrey Purinton's "Epicurus on the *Telos*" (1993) argues that the state of being free from pain is not itself a pleasure, but instead is the intentional object in which we take pleasure.

13. The virtues and philosophy

Ancient sources Epicurus *Ep. Men.* 122, 132 (IG I-4 122, 132; LS 25A, 21B); *KD* 5, 10–13 (IG I-5 5, 10–13; LS 21D, 25B); *SV* 27, 54 (IG I-6 27, 54; LS 25I1, 25D2); *DL* X 120 (IG I-8; LS 22Q); *DRN* I 62–79, III 1–30; Cic. *Fin.* I 34–6, 42–9; Stob. *Anthology* 3.17.33 (IG I-59); Ath. *Deipnosophists* 12, 547a (IG I-151); Porph. *To Marcella* 31 (IG I-124).

Martha Nussbaum's "Therapeutic Arguments: Epicurus and Aristotle" (1986) argues (from a broadly Aristotelian perspective) that the Epicureans take a strictly instrumental view of the value of arguments, and that this view has troubling implications. Pierre Hadot's *What is Ancient Philosophy*? (2002) contends that ancient philosophy is primarily a way of life instead of a system of theories. It includes extensive consideration of the Epicurean communities in chapter 7.

14. Justice

Ancient sources *KD* 6–7, 14, 31–40 (IG I-5 6–7, 14, 31–40; LS 22C1, 22a, 22B1–2, 22C2); *SV* 51, 58 (IG I-6 58; LS 21G3, 22D1); *DL* X 117–20 (IG I-8; LS 22Q); *DRN* V 925–1135 (LS 22K, 19B, 22L); Cic. *Fin.* I 50–53; Porp. *Abst.* I.44.2–I.55.4, I.7.1–12.7 (LS 22M–N); Stob. *Anthology* 4.143 (IG I-154).

Paul Vander Waerdt's "Hermarchus and the Epicurean Genealogy of Morals" (1988) is a good introduction to Hermarchus' account of the origin of justice (as preserved in Porphyry), an understudied text. Vander Waerdt argues that Hermarchus adapts the Stoic doctrine of *oikeiosis*, a natural kinship between members of the same species, to help explain the origin of justice and the exclusion of animals from the justice contract, and that in so doing Hermarchus enriches the basic Epicurean doctrine. John Armstrong's "Epicurean Justice" (1997) contains a nice discussion of how justice as a virtue relates to justice as a property of social institutions.

15. Friendship

Ancient sources *KD* 27, 40 (IG I-5 27, 40; LS 22E, 22C2); *SV* 34, 39, 52, 56–7, 66, 78 (IG I-6 34, 39, 52, 56-57, 66, 78; LS 22F3, 22F4, 22F5, 22F6, 22F7); *DL* X 120–21 (IG I-8; LS 22Q); Cic. *Fin.* I 65–70 (IG I-26; LS 22O), II 78–85; Sen. *Ep.* 9.8 (IG I-54).

Matt Evans's "Can Epicureans Be Friends?" (2004) answers "yes" to the title's question, and provides an extended and convincing argument that the Epicurean position on friendship can be reconciled with their hedonism. Voula Tsouna's *The Ethics of Philodemus* (2007) is a wide-ranging reconstruction of the ethics of this later Epicurean, who was an important source of information for Cicero. Among many other topics, such as Philodemus on property management, Tsouna argues that Philodemus was most probably the source for the "timid" revisionist account of friendship that Torquatus lays out in *On Ends*, so that Philodemus was the source of one of the most important modifications of Epicurean orthodoxy.

16. The gods

Ancient sources Epicurus *Ep. Men.* 123–4 (IG I-4 123–4; LS 23B), 135 (IG I-4 135; LS 23J); *KD* 1 (IG I-5 1; LS 23E4); *DRN* II 600–660, III 1–30, V 146–55 (LS 23L), VI

68–79 (LS 23D); Cic. *Nat. D.* I 43–56 (IG I-16; LS 23E), 69–76 (IG I-17); Sext. Emp. *Math.* IX 43–7 (LS 23F); Phld. *On piety* 105 (IG I-56), 112.5–12 (LS 23H).

M. Erler's "Epicurus as *dues mortalis: Homoiosis theoi* and Epicurean Self-cultivation" (2002) examines Epicurus himself as an instantiation of the Epicurean ideal of "becoming godlike", as Lucretius describes him, and argues that this Epicurean doctrine is rooted in similar ideas put forward in Plato's *Timaeus*. André-Jean Festugière's short book *Epicurus and his Gods* (1955) does not much engage with the questions that have dominated most of this chapter, about the exact ontological status of the gods. Instead, it places Epicurean religious practices within the contexts of religious practices of the day and the ways in which members of Epicurean communities embody the Epicurean ideals of friendship.

17. Death

Ancient sources Epicurus *Ep. Men.* 124–5 (IG I-4 124–5; LS 24A); *KD* 19–21 (IG I-5 19–21; LS 24C); *SV* 14 (IG I-6 14); *DRN* III 630–1094 (LS 14G, 14H, 24E, 24F, 24G); Plut. *Non posse* 1101a–b (IG I-40); Phld. *On Death* XXV 2–10.

Warren's *Facing Death* (2004) is an excellent book that tries to bridge the gap between the modern discussions of the harmfulness of death and the Epicurean texts that inspire those discussions. It is hard to overestimate the impact that Thomas Nagel's admirably short, clear and provocative article "Death" (1979) has had on subsequent discussions of the Epicurean arguments concerning death. Nagel's article is also included in John Fischer's *The Metaphysics of Death* (1993), an outstanding compilation of articles dealing with death, most inspired by the Epicurean arguments.

Bibliography

Annas, J. 1993a. *The Morality of Happiness*. Oxford: Oxford University Press.

Annas, J. 1993b. "Epicurus on Agency". In *Passions and Perceptions: Studies in Hellenistic Philosophy of Mind, Proceedings of the 5th Symposium Hellenisticum*, J. Brunschwig & M. Nussbaum (eds), 53–71. Cambridge: Cambridge University Press.

Annas, J. (ed.) 2001. *Cicero: On Moral Ends*, R. Woolf (trans.). Cambridge: Cambridge University Press.

Arenson, K. 2009. *Pleasure and the Absence of Pain: Reading Epicurus' Hedonism Through Plato's* Philebus. PhD dissertation, Emory University.

Armstrong, J. 1997. "Epicurean Justice". *Phronesis* **42**: 324–34.

Asmis, E. 1984. *Epicurus' Scientific Method.* Ithaca, NY: Cornell University Press.

Asmis, E. 1990. "Free Action and the Swerve". *Oxford Studies in Ancient Philosophy* **8**: 275–90.

Atherton, C. 2007. "Reductionism, Rationality and Responsibility: A Discussion of Tim O'Keefe, *Epicurus on Freedom*". *Archiv für Geschichte der Philosophie* **89**: 192–230.

Bailey, C. [1928] 1964. *The Greek Atomists and Epicurus.* New York: Russell and Russell.

Bailey, C. 1947. *Titi Lvcreti Cari: De Rervm Natvra: Libri Sex.* Oxford: Clarendon Press.

Brunschwig, J. 1986. "The Cradle Argument in Epicureanism and Stoicism". In *The Norms of Nature*, M. Schofield & G. Striker (eds), 113–44. Cambridge: Cambridge University Press.

Burnyeat, M. 1978. "The Upside-down Back-to-front Sceptic of Lucretius IV 472". *Philologus* **122**: 197–206.

Burnyeat, M. 1980. "Can the Sceptic Live his Scepticism?". In *Doubt and Dogmatism*, J. Barnes, M. Burnyeat & M. Schofield (eds), 20–53. Oxford: Oxford University

Press. Reprinted in *The Original Sceptics: A Controversy*, M. Burnyeat & M. Frede (eds), 25–57 (Indianapolis, IN: Hackett, 1998).

Cambiano, G. 1999. "Philosophy, Science and Medicine". In *The Cambridge History of Hellenistic Philosophy*, K. Algra (ed.), 585–613. Cambridge: Cambridge University Press.

Campbell, G. 2003. *Lucretius on Creation and Evolution*. Oxford: Oxford University Press.

Chisholm, R. [1964] 1982. "Human Freedom and the Self". Reprinted in *Free Will*, G. Watson (ed.), 7–29. Oxford: Oxford University Press.

Clay, D. 1998. *Paradosis and Survival: Three Chapters in the History of Epicurean Philosophy*. Ann Arbor, MI: University of Michigan Press.

Cooper, J. 1998. "Pleasure and Desire in Epicurus". In his *Reason and Emotion: Essays on Ancient Moral Psychology and Ethical Theory*, 485–514. Princeton, NJ: Princeton University Press.

Curd, P. 1997. *The Legacy of Parmenides: Eleatic Monism and Later Presocratic Thought*. Princeton, NJ: Princeton University Press.

Curd, P. 2001. "Why Democritus Was Not a Skeptic". In *Essays in Ancient Greek Philosophy, Vol. 6: Before Plato*, A. Preus (ed.), 149–69. Albany, NY: SUNY Press.

De Lacey, P. & E. De Lacey (trans.) 1978. *Philodemus, On Methods of Inference*, 2nd edn. Naples: Bibliopolis.

Englert, W. 1987. *Epicurus on the Swerve and Voluntary Action*. Atlanta, GA: Scholar's Press.

Erler, M. 2002. "Epicurus as *dues mortalis: Homoiosis theoi* and Epicurean Self-cultivation". In *Traditions of Theology*, D. Frede & A. Laks (eds), 159–81. Leiden: Brill.

Evans, M. 2004. "Can Epicureans Be Friends?" *Ancient Philosophy* **24**: 407–24.

Festugière, A. 1955. *Epicurus and his Gods*. Oxford: Basil Blackwell.

Fischer, J. (ed.) 1993. *The Metaphysics of Death*. Stanford, CA: Stanford University Press.

Fowler, D. 2002. *Lucretius on Atomic Motion: A Commentary on* De rerum natura *2.1–332*. Oxford: Oxford University Press.

Furley, D. 1967. *Two Studies in the Greek Atomists*. Princeton, NJ: Princeton University Press.

Furley, D. 1981. "The Greek Theory of the Infinite Universe". *Journal of the History of Ideas* **42**: 571–85.

Furley, D. 1989a. *Cosmic Problems: Essays on Greek and Roman Philosophy of Nature*. Cambridge: Cambridge University Press.

Furley, D. 1989b. "Aristotle and the Atomists on Motion in a Void". See Furley (1989a), 77–90.

Furley, D. 1989c. "Weight and Motion in Democritus' Theory". See Furley (1989a), 91–102.

Furley, D. 1993. "Democritus and Epicurus on Sensible Qualities". In *Passions and Perceptions*, J. Brunschwig & M. Nussbaum (eds), 72–94. Cambridge: Cambridge University Press.

Ganson, T. 1999. "Democritus against Reducing Sensible Qualities". *Ancient Philosophy* **19**: 201–15.

Gosling, J. & C. Taylor 1982. *The Greeks on Pleasure*. Oxford: Oxford University Press.

Grice, P. 1957. "Meaning". *Philosophical Review* **65**: 141–58.

Hadot, P. 2002. *What is Ancient Philosophy*? Cambridge, MA: Harvard University Press.

Hankinson, R. 1995. *The Sceptics*. London: Routledge.

Hankinson, R. 1998. *Cause and Explanation in Ancient Greek Thought*. Oxford: Oxford University Press.

Huby, P. 1967. "The First Discovery of the Freewill Problem". *Philosophy* **42**: 353–62.

Hume, D. 1985. *Essays: Moral Political, and Literary*, rev. edn. Indianapolis, IN: Liberty Fund.

Humphries, R. (trans.) 1968. *Lucretius: The Way Things Are. The De Rerum Natura of Titus Lucretius Carus*. Bloomington, IN: Indiana University Press.

Inwood, B. & L. Gerson 1994. *The Epicurus Reader: Selected Writings and Testimonia*. Indianapolis. IN: Hackett.

Inwood, B. & L. Gerson 1997. *Hellenistic Philosophy: Introductory Readings*, 2nd edn. Indianapolis, IN: Hackett.

Kontan, D., D. Clay & C. Glad (ed. & trans.) 1998. *Philodemus: On Frank Criticism*. Atlanta, GA: Society of Biblical Literature.

Kripke, S. 1980. *Naming and Necessity*. Cambridge, MA: Harvard University Press.

Laursen, S. 1995. "The Early Parts of Epicurus *On Nature* 25th Book". *Cronache Ercolanesi* **25**: 5–109.

Laursen, S. 1997. "The Later Parts of Epicurus *On Nature* 25th Book". *Cronache Ercolanesi* **27**: 5–82.

Lee, M. 2005. *Epistemology after Protagoras: Responses to Relativism in Plato, Aristotle, and Democritus*. Oxford: Oxford University Press.

Long, A. A. & D. N. Sedley 1987. *The Hellenistic Philosophers*, 2 vols. Cambridge: Cambridge University Press.

Mackie, J. L. 1982. *The Miracle of Theism*. Oxford: Clarendon Press.

Mitsis, P. 1988. *Epicurus' Ethical Theory: The Pleasures of Invulnerability*. Ithaca, NY: Cornell University Press.

Nagel, T. 1979. "Death". In his *Mortal Questions*, 1–10. Cambridge: Cambridge University Press. Originally published in *Noûs* **4** (1970): 73–80.

Nussbaum, M. 1986. "Therapeutic Arguments: Epicurus and Aristotle". In *The Norms of Nature*, M. Schofield & G. Striker (eds), 31–74. Cambridge: Cambridge University Press.

O'Brien, D. 1981. *Theories of Weight in the Ancient World: Four Essays on Democritus, Plato and Aristotle. A Study in the Development of Ideas. Volume One: Democritus, Weight and Size: An Exercise in the Reconstruction of Early Greek Philosophy*. Paris: Les Belles Lettres.

O'Connor, D. 1989. "The Invulnerable Pleasures of Epicurean Friendship". *Greek, Roman, and Byzantine Studies* **30**: 165–86.

O'Keefe, T. 1996. "Does Epicurus Need the Swerve as an *Archê* of Collisions?" *Phronesis* **41**: 305–17.

O'Keefe, T. 1997. "The Ontological Status of Sensible Qualities for Democritus and Epicurus". *Ancient Philosophy* **17**: 119–34.

O'Keefe, T. 2001a. "Would a Society of Wise Epicureans Be Just?" *Ancient Philosophy* **21**: 133–46.

O'Keefe, T. 2001b. "Is Epicurean Friendship Altruistic?" *Apeiron* **34**: 269–305.

O'Keefe, T. 2003. "Lucretius on the Cycle of Life and the Fear of Death". *Apeiron* **36**: 43–65.

O'Keefe, T. 2005. *Epicurus on Freedom*. Cambridge: Cambridge University Press.

O'Keefe, T. 2006. Review of Warren, *Facing Death* (2004). *Ancient Philosophy* **26**: 430–35.

O'Keefe, T. 2009. "Action and Responsibility". In *The Cambridge Companion to Epicureanism*, J. Warren (ed.), 142–57. Cambridge: Cambridge University Press.

Parfit, D. 1971. "Personal Identity". *Philosophical Review* **80**: 3–27.

Parfit, D. 1984. *Reasons and Persons*. Oxford: Oxford University Press.

Pasnau, R. 2007. "Democritus and Secondary Qualities". *Archiv für Geschichte der Philosophie* **89**: 99–121.

Purinton, J. 1993. "Epicurus on the *Telos*". *Phronesis* **38**: 281–320.

Purinton, J. 1999. "Epicurus on 'Free Volition' and the Atomic Swerve". *Phronesis* **44**: 253–99.

Sedley, D. 1982. "Two Conceptions of Vacuum". *Phronesis* **27**: 175–93.

Sedley, D. 1983. "Epicurus' Refutation of Determinism". In *Suzètèsis: Studi sull'epicureismo greco e romano offerti a M. Gigante*, vol. I, 11–51. Naples: Bibliopolis.

Sedley, D. 1988. "Epicurean Anti-Reductionism". In *Matter and Metaphysics*, J. Barnes & M. Mignucci (eds), 295–327. Naples: Bibliopolis.

Sedley, D. 1989. "Philosophical Allegiance in the Greco-Roman World". In *Philosophia Togata*, M. Griffin & J. Barnes (eds), 97–119. Oxford: Oxford University Press.

Sedley, D. 1998a. *Lucretius and the Transformation of Greek Wisdom*. Cambridge: Cambridge University Press.

Sedley, D. 1998b. "The Inferential Foundations of Epicurean Ethics". In *Ethics*, S. Everson (ed.), 129–50. Cambridge: Cambridge University Press.

Smith, M. (ed. & trans.) 1993. *Diogenes of Oinoanda: The Epicurean Inscription*. Naples: Bibliopolis.

Smith, M. 1998. "Excavations at Oinoanda: the New Epicurean Texts". *Anatolian Studies* **48**: 125–70.

Smith, M. 2001. *Lucretius: On the Nature of Things*. Indianapolis, IN: Hackett.

Stallings, A. (trans.) 2007. *Lucretius: The Nature of Things*. Harmondsworth: Penguin.

Strahm, M. 2009. *Epicurean Friendship: How are Friends Pleasurable?* Master's thesis, Georgia State University.

Striker, G. 1993. "Epicurean Hedonism". In *Passions and Perceptions*, J. Brunschwig & M. Nussbaum (eds), 3–17. Cambridge: Cambridge University Press. Reprinted in her *Essays on Hellenistic Epistemology and Ethics*, 196–208 (Cambridge: Cambridge University Press, 1996).

Striker, G. 1996. "Epicurus on the Truth of Sense-impressions". In her *Essays on Hellenistic Epistemology and Ethics*, 77–91. Cambridge: Cambridge University Press.

Taylor, C. 1999. *The Atomists: Leucippus and Democritus. Fragments: A Text and Translation with a Commentary*. Toronto: University of Toronto Press.

Thorsrud, H. 2008. *Ancient Scepticism*. Stocksfield: Acumen.

Tsouna, V. 2007. *The Ethics of Philodemus*. Oxford: Oxford University Press.

van Inwagen, P. 1990. *Material Beings*. Ithaca, NY: Cornell University Press.

Vander Waerdt, P. 1988. "Hermarchus and the Epicurean Genealogy of Morals". *Transactions of the American Philological Association* **118**: 87–106.

Verlinsky, A. 2005. "Epicurus and his Predecessors on the Origins of Language". In *Language and Learning: Philosophy of Language in the Hellenistic Age*, D. Frede & B. Inwood (eds), 56–100. Cambridge: Cambridge University Press.

Wardy, R. 1988. "Eleatic Pluralism". *Archiv für Geschichte der Philosophie* **70**: 125–46.

Warren, J. 2004. *Facing Death: Epicurus and His Critics*. Oxford: Oxford University Press.

Warren, J. 2006. "Epicureans and the Present Past". *Phronesis* **51**: 362–87.

Warren, J. (ed.) 2009. *The Cambridge Companion to Epicureanism*. Cambridge: Cambridge University Press.

Woolf, R. 2004. "What Kind of Hedonist is Epicurus?" *Phronesis* **49**: 303–22.

Index